COMPLETE
WOMEN'S WEIGHT TRAINING
GUIDE

COMPLETE
WOMEN'S WEIGHT TRAINING
GUIDE

by Edie Leen

ANDERSON WORLD, INC.

Library of Congress Cataloging in Publication Data

Leen, Edie, 1959 -
    Complete women's weight training.

    Bibliography: p.
    Includes index.
    1. Weight lifting. 2. Physical fitness.
I. Title.
GV546.L43   796.4'1   78-64384
ISBN 0-89037-161-X

All photographs by David K. Madison

Second Printing, July 1981

*No information may be reprinted in any form
without permission from the publisher.*

Anderson World, Inc.
Mountain View, California

To Ed, with love

Contents

Acknowledgments

A "thank you" with much appreciation to everyone who helped with this book—I'm very grateful! Above all, I'd like to thank my husband Ed for his immeasurable support. Without him, it wouldn't have been possible.

Introduction

In recent years there has been much controversy regarding the use of progressive resistance exercise—weight training—by women. It is the purpose of this book to show how any woman can achieve, maintain, or regain health, strength, and beauty by following the authors' three-point program. It provides a comprehensive plan for feminine fitness through weight training, nutrition, and the use of mental preparation.

The ability of progressive resistance exercises to re-shape, firm, and redistribute body weight has been established. However, the role of nutrition and the development of new mental attitudes has been neglected. Developing new habits, following a proper diet, and *understanding why* enhance the body and add zest to the life of the woman who adopts this program.

Weight training offers something for everybody. The female athlete whose skill and technique are greater than her strength can develop muscular power to the point of ultimate performance in her chosen sport. Special exercises can erase figure problems where weight redistribution is the goal. Physical problems unique to women (e.g., lower backaches, menstrual pain) can be reduced and in some cases eliminated.

Every woman will find that the basic program presented here will give her a firmer body, greater agility, better co-ordination, and more stamina. The female hormones prevent an overly muscular look—a fear of some women.

One must be realistic when beginning a long-range program. It is better to set a series of goals, work towards them, and establish new ones as you progress. Your body will respond much better if you begin slowly. Conversely, if you try to do too much too soon, your body will resist and you'll become discouraged.

The woman who embarks on a weight training program can be her own success story. A routine checkup with a physician will reveal any limitations or restrictions. Even so, progressive resistance exercises are so varied and so individual that a program can be devised for anyone.

Before starting, read the book. Mark any sentence or paragraph that applies to your own goals with a pencil, to be referred to later. The key to success is good nutrition and, most important, motivation. Be honest with yourself. It may be an advantage not to confide your plans to others. After all, no one can train for you, no one else is on your team, and no one can do your exercises for you. But the personal satisfaction, the benefits, and the rewards belong only to you. The better bust, the smaller waist, the flatter tummy, and the firmer arms and legs belong only to the woman who has worked for them.

The desire to improve your body begins in your mind, and developing the proper mental attitude is the foundation of success. Good nutrition provides the energy that makes a program possible. Selecting and sticking to proper series of exercises guarantees the final achievement of your individual goal.

1

Getting Started

This chapter presents some important tips on getting your weight training started correctly. It covers a lot of basic questions that you might have doubt about. Addressing these questions in the beginning should be helpful, and should enable you to save a lot of time and money and be more enthusiastic!

CHOOSING THE RIGHT HEALTH CLUB

The most important thing to keep in mind when choosing a health club is that you must be completely comfortable with the atmosphere of the place. The club should be roomy, have good ventilation, and friendly, enthusiastic instructors and members. Next in importance is proper equipment, e.g., pulleys, dumbbells, and floor space. Try to avoid places that have numerous roller machines and that give body wraps. In addition your club should offer qualified instructors who are knowledgeable, enthusiastic, and willing to spend their time with you.

The last items to consider are the location and fees. The club should be easy to get to, with ample parking, and shouldn't require you to drive a great distance. All of these things will have an effect on your mental attitude. Most health clubs have reasonable rates, but you should avoid any long-term contracts and stay within your own price range.

1

WHEN TO TRAIN

Setting a regular time for your workouts usually results in more energetic and productive training programs. Most people, because of work or school, find it more convenient to exercise in the late afternoon or evening. Your schedule may require you to train at some other time, but you can obviously make good progress regardless of when you train.

I have discovered that the morning is when I have the most energy; my mind is clear and best suited to get the most out of my exercise program. So I work out first thing in the morning before doing anything else. Another important question is: how soon after eating is it good to exercise? The best time is about one hour before you eat or two hours after a full meal.

CLOTHING

The most important factor about the clothes that you work out in is that they must be comfortable. Be sure to wear clothing that will allow you to move freely without any restriction. I have found leotards and tights to be best for me. Besides being comfortable, they allow me to see my figure while exercising. I find that this helps to motivate and inspire me in my workouts, and lets me see what areas need work. I can also check for any improvements in my figure.

It's also a good idea, but not mandatory, to wear shoes that give your feet support, such as tennis shoes. Sweat clothes, T-shirts, and shorts are also good to work out in. Just remember, when buying your gym clothes, that they should be loose-fitting and comfortable, not just fashionable ones! You are supposed to build a better body, not a better wardrobe!

UNDERSTANDING SETS AND REPS

A weight training program is made up of different exercises grouped into sequence by a system of *sets* and *reps*. A *rep* is one repetition of an exercise. All reps should be performed using a smooth continuous movement. A *set* is a pre-determined number of repetitions of a single exercise. All sets of a given exercise should be performed before continuing on to the next exercise.

An example of the set and rep system would be two sets of ten reps (2 x 10). This means that you perform a given exercise ten times (repetitions), rest for about a minute, and then perform another ten repetitions of the same exercise.

PROPER BREATHING

How to breathe properly when exercising is one of the most common questions asked. You should learn to breathe correctly from the beginning of your training by following the procedure explained here.

The basic principle is to inhale while your body is under the least amount of stress, and exhale while you are performing against resistance. It is important to learn proper breathing; once you have, it will become easy and you will do it naturally. Be sure *not* to hold your breath when exercising, because your breathing is what sends oxygen to your muscles, enabling them to work.

The time you rest between sets is determined by your endurance. You should only rest between sets long enough to allow your breathing to return to normal. As you progress in your training program, you will find that your endurance will increase and the time you need to rest between sets will decrease.

PHYSICAL EXAM

Before starting your weight training or any program of physical activity, it is a good idea to get a complete physical examination from your physician. There is no inherent age limit on physical improvement by regular exercise. Your doctor will most likely give you a clean bill of health, but if you do have any health problems, he or she can correct them before you start your training program. Your doctor may also have some very useful advice to help make your exercise routine more beneficial to you.

If you are in reasonably good health and already physically active, you can probably go right into a training program, but be sure to ease into it, and progress gradually. If any problems should occur, consult your physician.

If you are not physically active, or if you haven't been for a long time, you must start slowly and cautiously, with

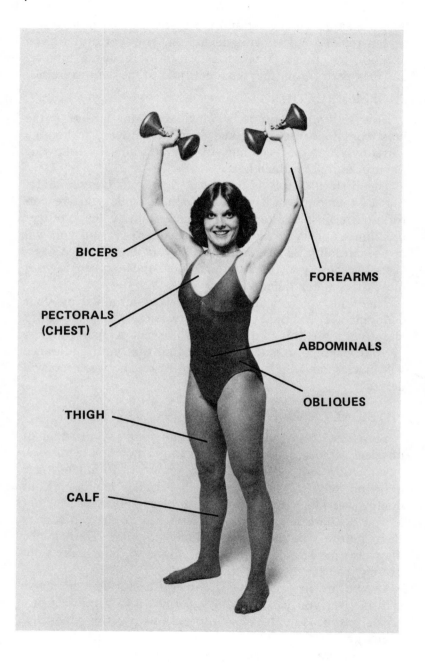

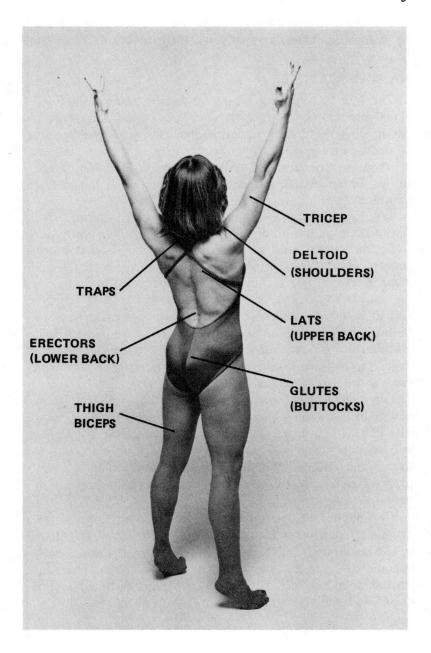

TRICEP

DELTOID
(SHOULDERS)

TRAPS

LATS
(UPPER BACK)

ERECTORS
(LOWER BACK)

GLUTES
(BUTTOCKS)

THIGH
BICEPS

just a few exercises. This will allow your body to get adjusted to exercising. Then, gradually work up to your full weight training program.

MENTAL ATTITUDE

The way to achieve a successful weight training and nutritional program is to develop your motivation and desire to get in shape—and keep it. Remember that you have decided to do something good for yourself! Remember too that you are training for yourself, not for others. Sure it's nice to receive compliments, but personal satisfaction is the greatest compliment of all.

Try to avoid any negative ideas that will have an effect on you and your training. You must be positive about yourself, your work, and your personal habits. Success breeds success. Start by improving every day in little things that mean a lot. Do not set unrealistic goals for yourself that are impossible to achieve. Take a good, honest look at yourself and then build an exercise and nutritional program that will be both realistic and challenging. Be sure to take into consideration your height, bone structure, work schedule, and any other factors that could affect your program. Set attainable goals and begin by taking one step at a time.

The best way to change your eating habits is to develop new habits in such a way that they will become part of you. The person who loses ten to fifteen pounds by crash dieting will probably gain it back quickly because they go back to the eating patterns that made them overweight in the first place. Teaching yourself how to eat correctly is the only permanent way to weight control.

This applies in the same way to exercise. Some people decide to start exercising, but they jump into it so hard in the beginning that they ruin the true benefits and usually become discouraged and quit. Keep in mind that everyone started as a beginner; follow the programs outlined in this book and remember to be realistic in your goals.

2

Warm-Up and Cool-Down

Warming up is the ideal way to prepare the body for exercise. Your pulse rate should be increased gradually until the heart and circulatory system raise your body temperature and get the blood flowing through the entire body. An appropriate warm-up will make your muscles more flexible and responsive to exercise, as well as help to prevent injuries. It will also leave you feeling physically and mentally ready to get started on your weight training program.

There are numerous warm-up exercises, so choose two or three that suit your individual needs and develop a warm-up routine that lasts five to ten minutes. Remember, this is a time to tune yourself in, both mentally and physically, to your body. Training without first warming up is only inviting injury and less-than-maximum results.

BEND AND REACH

This exercise warms up your whole body, preparing you for the rest of your exercises. Begin by standing with your feet slightly wider than shoulder width apart. Arms are stretched up straight over your head and thumbs are interlocked together (Photo 1). Now, bend your knees as you swing your arms down, pushing them straight through your legs. This is done all in one smooth movement (Photo 2). Bring your arms back up and straighten your legs to your starting position and repeat. Begin slowly, to get familiar with the movement, and gradually work up to a fast pace.

Photo 1   Photo 2

MODIFIED SIDE BENDS

This is a great all-purpose warm-up and also helps to trim your waist at the same time. Stand with your feet a comfortable distance apart, with your right arm circled over your head, and the left one circled downward in front of your body. Both arms are slightly bent at the elbow (Photo 3). Now begin a swinging movement by bending at your waist, while exchanging the position of your arms. Bend as far as possible to your right side with your left arm overhead (Photo 4).

Then bend to your right side as far as possible, with your left arm circled over your head. This exercise should be done in a smooth, continuous movement.

Be sure you bend far enough to feel a good stretch along your side. Gradually build up to a fast pace.

JUMPING JACKS

Jumping jacks are good for toning the body as well as increasing circulation, allowing you to get warmed up quickly. To begin, stand with your feet together and your arms straight down at sides (Photo 5). Start this movement by jumping outward, spreading your legs slightly wider than

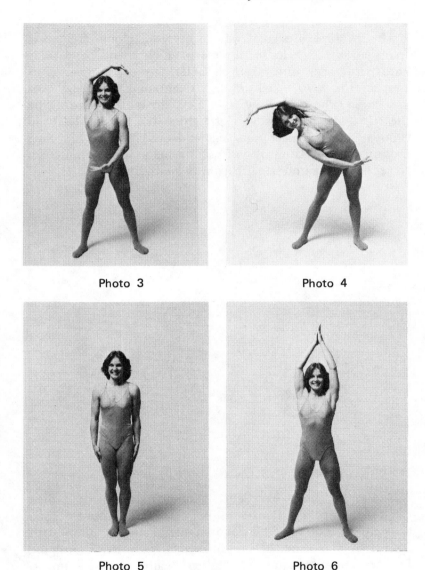

Photo 3   Photo 4

Photo 5   Photo 6

shoulder width, and, at the same time, bring your arms straight over your head with the palms together (Photo 6). Return to starting position and repeat.

Begin slowly, until your coordination gets better and the movement becomes easy; then pick up the pace.

BICYCLING

This exercise is a great way to get your blood circulating and your muscles loose. Lie on your back and bend your knees; roll back onto your shoulders, using your hands to support the lower back while straightening your legs over your head (Photo 7). Now make a cycling motion by drawing the right leg down as you straighten the left leg back up (Photo 8). Exchange your legs and continue the bicycling motion. Be sure to move your legs rapidly and continuously to get the maximum benefit from this movement.

Photo 7   Photo 8

JUMPING ROPE AND RUNNING IN PLACE

These are both excellent warm-up movements which can help prepare your body for the rest of your routine, as well as increase your endurance. You can jump with both feet at a time, or one foot at a time. Begin jumping for two minutes and increase gradually, working up to five minutes. Begin running in place at a moderate speed and then increase gradually. Run for one minute, and work up to five minutes.

STRETCHING

Stretches are a must if you are tight and out of shape—

beginners, take note! Unlike running or jumping rope, *static* stretches should be done slowly with each position held steadily for a slow count of ten. Such stretches are an excellent way to promote flexibility, which should be a high priority as you begin weight training programs.

The basic rule is to hold the position for a slow count of ten, and never bounce. Allow yourself to progress gradually to the point where you can assume the full position. Your capacity will increase with practice. Initially you can expect a bit of stiffness but a nice hot bath and a repeat of the exercises will help you recover. Do all stretches slowly.

Stretching will complement your warm-up routine and enhance your workout performance. The added flexibility achieved through stretching exercises will help you make greater progress in your program. Stretching exercises are not done like other movements, but by slowly stretching into a certain position, and holding it, while trying to relax the muscles involved. It is of the utmost importance to allow yourself to progress gradually and not force yourself into any of these positions. Just because you may not be able to assume the full position right away doesn't mean you're not benefiting. Your muscles will increase their stretching capacity with practice, to the point where you can assume the full position. Another important rule to remember is never to bounce yourself into a position. This is the most common mistake and invites injury!

Add five to ten minutes of stretching exercises after your warm-ups to help increase muscle flexibility and range of movement, both of which are vital to your weight training program.

OVERHEAD STRETCH

The overhead stretch is a great exercise for limbering up the whole body. Begin by standing with your feet slightly apart, and arms overhead. (Photo 11). Stretch up, reaching as high as possible with your right hand and lift up onto your toes at the same time. Now reach slowly with your other hand, stretching as high as you can. You should bring both arms up high, and stay up on your toes! Bring feet and arms down and rest for a few seconds, then repeat entire exercise.

Photo 11

WISHBONE STRETCH

Begin by sitting on the floor with your back straight and legs spread as wide apart as you can keep them without straining. Your arms are resting in front of you (Photo 12). Now, with feet pointed, reach down slowly and try to grasp your right ankle with both hands, pulling body forward. Attempt to stretch beyond your knee with your chin, and hold this position for a count of ten (Photo 13). Slowly return to an upright position and repeat on the left side. Repeat the same exercise, only keep your feet flexed this time.

Be sure to begin slowly and as you progress, work on opening your legs wider, and reaching farther down your leg with chin.

INNER THIGH STRETCH

This is an excellent exercise for stretching your inner thigh muscles, and will help to increase flexibility in your legs. Begin by sitting on the floor with your back straight.

Photo 12　　　　　　　　Photo 13

Bend legs at the knees, bringing the soles of your feet together and pulled in close to your body. Grasp your feet while trying to keep the knees as close to the floor as you can (Photo 14).

Keeping your back straight, slowly lower your body forward with chin up and neck stretched, and attempt to touch your chest to your feet; hold for about ten seconds (Photo 15). Slowly bring yourself to an upright position and repeat.

This is a difficult one, so be sure to begin slowly and only lower your body forward as much as you can without straining. Each time you will be able to lean forward a little farther. Remember not to bounce!

CALF STRETCH

This exercise is great for stretching your calf muscles and will also improve their flexibility.

Begin by placing a sturdy chair or stool about two feet in front of you. With your right leg forward lean on the back of the chair with body weight on hands and feet (Photo 16). Now lunge forward, bending right leg and at the elbows. Left leg remains straight and heels are kept flat on the floor at all times. Hold for a count of ten (Photo 17). Repeat with left leg forward.

If you don't feel a good stretch, try moving further away from the chair. Remember to keep feet flat on the floor at all times.

Photo 14

Photo 15

Photo 16

Photo 17

FORWARD STRETCH

This is an excellent movement for increasing flexibility in your legs, hips, and back. Sit on the floor with your legs together and straight, directly in front of you; keep your back straight and toes pointed (Photo 18). Slowly grasp your ankles (as far down the leg as possible), and pull your upper body forward. Keeping your chin up and neck stretched, try to touch your stomach to your thighs. Hold position for a few seconds (Photo 19). Now repeat the exercise, only this time keep your feet flexed (Photo 20) and your head up.

Be sure to lower your body down only as far as you can without straining, and gradually work on getting down a little further each time. Remember, do not bounce!

Photo 18, upper left
Photo 19, upper right
Photo 20, bottom

SIDE STRETCH

The side stretch is great for the entire upper body, especially your waistline. Begin with your feet comfortably apart and arms overhead, with the right hand holding on to your left wrist (Photo 21). Slowly bend to the right side, gently pulling the left arm over so you can feel a good stretch all along your left side; pause (Photo 22). Return to starting position and repeat stretch on your left side, reversing your hands.

This is a side stretch, so don't bend forward! Also remember to keep buttocks tucked under and your hips forward.

Photo 21   Photo 22

COOL DOWN

Cooling down is an important part of your total program. Just as your body needs a chance to warm up, it also needs to cool down, to lower the pulse rate, as well as body temperatures. Cooling down movements are light stretching exercises that don't involve much strain or effort. These exercises will return the body's temperature back to normal and help you avoid any unpleasant after-effects from training, such as cramps or dizziness.

The following are exercises that you can use to help cool down your body. Be sure to allow yourself these few minutes after each workout to adjust before going on with your daily activitites.

HEAD ROLLS

Head rolls are an excellent relaxation exercise, in addition to helping strengthen your neck and give it more flexibility. Begin by sitting in a comfortable position on the floor, with your head straight, and concentrate on relaxing your shoulders Drop your head downward and slowly roll to your right shoulder (Photo 23). Now make a half-circle as your roll your head to your left shoulder, and drop your head back. Continue rolling your head until desired number of reps are completed.

Photo 23

LUNGE AND STRETCH

This exercise is excellent for stretching the backs of your legs and your neck. It helps to firm your buttocks, too! Start this movement in a lunge position, with your right knee up to chest and your left leg stretched straight back. Your weight is resting on the balls of your feet, hands are flat on the floor, and your head is up (Photo 24). Slowly raise your buttocks as you straighten both your legs (knees locked) and at the same time, tuck your head in, stretching chin beyond your knee (Photo 25). Hold for a count of ten. Now lunge back down, returning to the starting position, and repeat. Be sure to stretch the leg in back as far as you can, in order to get a full stretch.

Photo 24

Photo 25

GRAVITY HANG

Stand up straight with feet comfortably apart. Bend forward at the waist and hang loosely. The force of gravity will pull your upper body down, closer to the floor. Once you are relaxed and comfortable, let your body sway back and forth, slowly; you should feel a pull in the back of your legs (Photo 26).

ARM STRETCHES

Stand with your feet slightly apart and raise arms over

your head. Reach with one arm, stretching up as high as possible, then reach slowly with the other arm. This will help to release any tightness in the upper body as you relax and slowly cool down (Photo 27).

TOE TOUCH

Stand with feet together and bend forward from the waist; as you stretch down slowly, try to touch the floor with your palms (Photo 28).

Photo 26

Photo 27

Photo 28

SLOW STRETCHES

Any of the slow warm-up stretches, such as the forward stretch, head rolls, or the wishbone stretch are good for cooling down. Do these with only light stretching and very slowly—remember, you're trying to relax and cool down!

ADVANCED STRETCHING

Here are a few more stretching exercises which are considered more advanced movements. You should try to do these every day at first, but once you have mastered them two or three times a week will be sufficient. As you progress, these stretches will become easier and you will find that they are excellent for relaxation.

Be careful not to exceed your level of flexibility too soon. Each time you try these movements, gradually attempt to get farther into the advanced position. Be sure to remember not to bounce in order to achieve these positions. Instead, pull slowly, stretch, and hold without moving.

Patience and consistency are the key factors to advanced stretching, for it will take time to master these positions, as well as to increase the length of time you'll be able to hold them.

LEG STRETCH

Begin by sitting on the floor with the soles of your feet together, keeping your back straight and hands resting on feet (Photo 29). Grasp the arch of your right foot with right hand, and slowly stretch leg up and out to the side as far as possible; try to straighten leg out all the way, locking your knee (Photo 30). Hold this position for a count of ten, and slowly bring leg down to starting position; repeat on your left leg. Continue alternating legs until desired number of reps are completed.

Don't try to straighten leg all the way unless you are very flexible. Instead, extend it only as far as is comfortable, even if your leg is bent at first. Gradually work on stretching your thigh and calf muscles, and it will come.

Photo 29

Photo 30

THE BRIDGE

Lie on your back with your hands flat on the floor alongside your head. Bend your knees while keeping feet on the floor close to buttocks (Photo 31).

Push your body upward by extending elbows and knees, and arching your back; keep head tucked under (Photo 32).

Photo 31

Photo 32

As you advance in this exercise, begin to move your feet and hands closer together to achieve a high arch and try to get up on your toes if possible.

BENDING STRETCH

Start by clasping your hands behind your back while keeping them straight (Photo 33). Slowly raise your arms as high as you can while standing up straight. Then, bend forward at the waist and stretch clasped hands overhead (Photo 34). Hold this position for a count of ten and slowly return to your starting position; then repeat.

Be sure to keep your legs straight throughout the movement, as this will enhance the stretch.

SITTING BACKBEND

Start by sitting on heels, with your hands resting at sides and your back straight (Photo 35). Slowly reach hands behind your body as far as you can comfortably. Drop your head back as you lift your chest. Raise your trunk and arch your back to form a backbend (Photo 36). Hold this position

Photo 33   Photo 34

Photo 35

Photo 36

for a count of ten. Return to starting position as you go backwards through the steps, and repeat.

Be sure to begin with only a few repetitions and gradually work up. As you progess in this movement, attempt gradually to place hands farther back behind you.

HALF BACKWARD SOMERSAULT

This exercise is an excellent way to stretch your legs, especially the backs of them, as well as your back and neck. Begin this movement by lying flat on your back with legs straight and together. Place your arms at your sides, with palms flat on the floor (Photo 37). Then, keeping legs and heels together and knees locked, roll over backwards (curving your whole body), until the balls of your feet are resting on the floor behind you, as close to your head as possible while keeping legs straight (Photo 38). Hold this position for a count of ten without moving. Slowly roll back to starting position.

Be sure to use a smooth movement throughout, and keep your legs straight. As you progress, move your feet closer to your head!

Photo 37   Photo 38

BENT-LEG SPLITS

This is a great way to achieve added flexibility in the backs of your legs.

Begin this movement by sitting on the floor in a hurdle

Photo 39   Photo 40

position with your left leg tucked back and right leg stretched open wide. Grasp your right leg as far down as possible as you slowly stretch body down, bringing chin beyond knee if possible, and hold (Photo 39).

While holding this position begin to straighten your left leg slowly as you work toward a full split position, keeping head down (Photo 40). Change legs and repeat.

Be sure not to bounce, but stretch slowly and try to concentrate on relaxing muscles involved in this movement.

3

Beginners Program

Enthusiasm for a new endeavor is fine, but for the beginner in weight training, determination and the desire to replace bad habits with new routines is vital.

The consequences of training too much at the start have caused many women to abandon a program before it gets off the ground. Keep in mind your reason for starting, and your exercises and diet will begin to reward your efforts. If you start slowly, your enthusiasm will increase instead of diminish.

During the first week of your program you should not work out with any heavy weights. Just concentrate on developing proper form and becoming comfortable with the exercises and equipment. The first few workouts should mostly be free-style exercise, or just one set per muscle group on the machines. Instead of worrying about your weak points, work through them and out of them. Concentrate on improving in general and avoid any downward pull of negative thinking.

Training should start with thirty minute workouts three times a week. Good nutrition, however, should be practiced three times a day, seven days a week.

KNEE-UP

This exercise tightens and flattens your stomach. It will also help to strengthen your lower back. Sit on the end of a flat bench, lean back, and support your body with your hands,

26

BEGINNERS PROGRAM

Exercises

| Warm-ups (pg. 7) | 5 - 10 minutes |
| Stretching (pg. 10) | 5 - 10 minutes |

Exercise	Sets	Reps	Weight
Stomach			
1. Knee-up (pg. 26)	1-2	10-15	0
Hips and Waist			
1. Bent-over twist (pg. 27)	1-2	10-15	0
Chest			
1. Bench press (pg. 29)	1-2	8-10	10
Shoulders			
1. Behind neck press (pg. 29)	1-2	8-10	10
Back			
1. Lat pull down (pg. 30)	1-2	8-10	10
Arms			
1. Barbell curl (pg. 32)	1-2	8-10	10
2. One-arm overhead extensions (pg. 32)	1-2	8-10	3-5
Legs			
1. Squat (pg. 33)	1-2	8-10	10
2. Single dumbbell calf raises (pg. 33)	1-2	10-15	5
Cool-down (pg. 16)	5 -10 minutes		

grasping both sides of the bench; keep legs extended straight out (Photo 41). Slowly bend your legs and pull knees up to chest (Photo 42). Then return to starting position and repeat.

Start with one or two sets of ten repetitions, and gradually work up to fifteen reps. Be sure to keep your stomach pulled in and toes pointed throughout exercise.

BENT-OVER TWIST

This exercise is great for trimming excess fat off the hips and waist, and helps increase flexibility in lower back.

Begin by standing with your feet about shoulder width apart; place an empty bar behind your neck and wrap your arms around it. With knees slightly bent, bend forward at the waist until your back is flat (Photo 43). Now twist at the waist to the right side, letting the end of the bar almost touch the floor (Photo 44). Then twist at the waist to your left side, again almost touching the floor with the end of the bar. Try one or two sets of ten reps, and aim for fifteen reps as you get more flexibile. Do not move your hips or head; they stay still as you twist. Begin slowly and gradually increase your speed. Keep correct form throughout the exercise.

Photo 41

Photo 42

Photo 43   Photo 44

BENCH PRESS

This excellent exercise will firm the entire chest area. It also will help strengthen and shape your shoulders, upper back, and arms.

Lie down on the bench and start with a light barbell at arms length, directly above your chest. Your hands should be slightly wider than shoulder width, using an overhand grip (Photo 46). Inhale deeply as you slowly lower the barbell straight down until it touches your mid-chest (Photo 47). Then press the weight back to extended position as you exhale. Begin with eight repetitions and slowly work up to ten. Be sure to use strict form in this movement, it's important that you concentrate on pushing with your chest muscles for best results.

BEHIND NECK PRESS

This exercise is excellent for shaping and strengthening your shoulders and arms. Begin in a standing position and grasp a light barbell with an overhand grip, at slightly wider than shoulder width. Keep you back straight and feet comfortably apart. Raise the barbell to a full overhead position

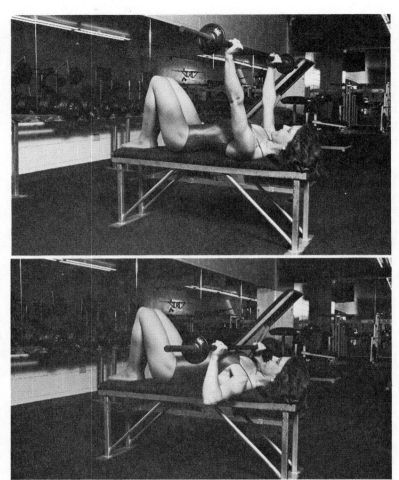

Photo 46, top;   Photo 47, bottom

(Photo 48). Begin slowly lowering the weight behind your head to the base of the neck (Photo 49). Press the barbell back to extended position and repeat.

Again, start with one set of eight repetitions and work up to two sets of ten. Keep your buttocks and stomach pulled in; this will help you to hold your body straight.

LAT PULL DOWN

This exercise will tone and strengthen your upper back. Begin by kneeling under the machine and grasp the bar with a wide overhand grip, arms fully extended (Photo 50). Slowly pull the bar down behind the head and pause (Photo 51). Gradually raise the bar back to extended position and repeat.

Eight repetitions are enough for starters; work up to two sets of ten reps. This exercise can be done to the front or back, whichever you prefer. Remember your breathing; inhale as you pull the bar down, and exhale as you raise it.

Also, do not bend forward at the waist; the upper body stays straight throughout the exercise.

Photo 48

Photo 49

Photo 50

Photo 51

BARBELL CURL

This exercise will tone and shape your biceps, the muscles at the front of your upper arms. Begin with your feet comfortably apart, and take a shoulder width underhand grip on a light barbell, resting it across your upper thighs (Photo 52). Keeping your elbows pinned to your sides, slowly curl the barbell upward toward your chin and pause (Photo 53). Lower the weight back to the starting position.

One set of barbell curls is sufficient; start with eight repetitions and work up to ten. It's important that you only use your upper arms to curl the weight, not your body. Also use a very light bar, as you don't want to build muscles, only tone them.

Photo 52   Photo 53

ONE-ARM OVERHEAD EXTENSION

This is an excellent exercise for firming the muscles at the back of your upper arm, the tricep. Start by standing with your feet comfortably apart and a light dumbbell held lightly in your right hand. Raise it to an overhead position (Photo 54). Gradually lower dumbbell behind the head to the base of the neck and pause (Photo 55). Push the dumbbell back to starting position and repeat until all reps are completed. Alternate with left arm.

One set of eight reps is how you should begin. It's important to keep your elbow back behind your head throughout this exercise. Also, if you prefer, you can do this exercise seated.

Photo 54   Photo 55

SQUAT

The squat is good for strengthening your thighs and knees. It also helps to firm and lift the buttocks. Place the barbell behind your head so it rests across your shoulders, and with your feet about twelve inches apart, place heels on a two inch block (Photo 56).

Slowly begin to lower yourself down until your thighs are parallel to the floor (Photo 57). Pause and raise yourself up to starting position and repeat.

One set of eight repetitions should be done at the start; work up to ten reps. Be sure to keep your body upright and back straight throughout the entire exercise. Inhale as you squat and exhale as you come back up.

SINGLE DUMBBELL CALF RAISES

This exercise will firm up your calves. Working one calf at a time, stand on a calf block with the toes and ball of your right foot resting on the edge, and heel hanging down as far as possible. Hold a light dumbbell in your right hand, balancing yourself with the left hand, and wrap your left leg around your right one (Photo 58). Rise up slowly onto your toes as high as possible (Photo 59) and then lower and return to starting position. Alternate with other calf.

One set of ten reps should be steadily increased until you can do fifteen of these calf raises. It's important to get the full movement by stretching at the bottom and rising up as high as possible!

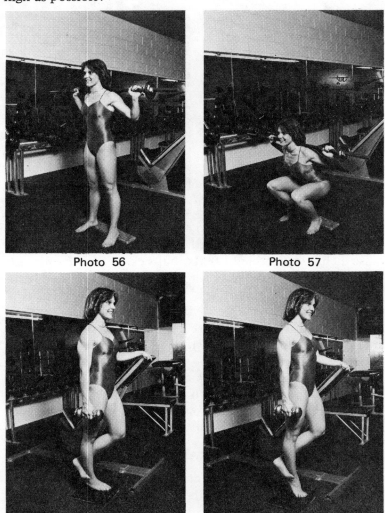

Photo 56   Photo 57

Photo 58   Photo 59

BEGINNER'S PROGRESS CHART

STARTING	1st WEEK	2nd WEEK	3rd WEEK	4th WEEK	5th WEEK	6th WEEK	7th WEEK	8th WEEK	NET LOSS
BODY WEIGHT									
BUSTLINE									
WAISTLINE									
HIPS									
THIGHS									
CALVES									
UPPER ARMS									

4

Intermediate Program

The most interesting phase of your weight training program is the Intermediate. With a proper mental attitude and your good nutrition, you have a new base for further development. Now you can concentrate on Progressive Resistance Exercises. Many women reach their original goals at the Intermediate level.

The Intermediate program will provide a wider variety of movements that will help you get quicker and more effective results. The beginner's program gave you an introduction to general body conditioning, which was a necessary foundation for the Intermediate program. If you practice the exercises outlined in this section consistently and correctly, they will help to firm and shape your entire body. This, in conjunction with proper diet, will rid your body of excess fat.

Like the beginner's program, this is a three-times-a-week program, but it has additional exercises, and you should be able to move through it at a faster pace.

LEG RAISES

Leg raises are excellent for your lower abdomen. Lying down on a flat bench, support your upper body by holding on to the sides of the bench. Your buttock at the end of the bench should be almost hanging off; keep your legs together and knees slightly bent, legs up in vertical position (Photo 60). Now, slowly move your legs as low as you can (Photo 61). Return to starting position and repeat.

Start with two sets of fifteen reps each, and work up to a point where you can do three sets of twenty-five reps. Be sure to do this exercise without pause.

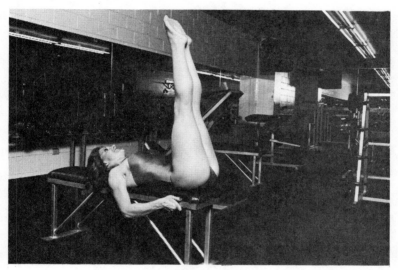

Photo 60

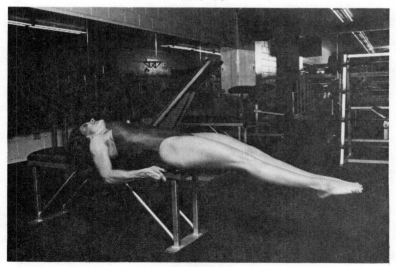

Photo 61

INTERMEDIATE PROGRAM

Exercises

Warm-up (pg. 7)	5 - 10 minutes
Stretching (pg. 10)	5 - 10 minutes

Exercises	Sets	Reps	Weight
Stomach			
1. Knee-up (pg. 26)	2-3	15-25	0
2. Leg raises (pg. 36)	2-3	15-25	0
Hip and Waist			
1. Bent-over twists (pg. 27)	2	25-50	0
2. Rear leg swing (pg. 38)	2	10-20	0
Chest			
1. Bench press (pg. 29)	2-3	10-12	10-15
2. Incline flys (pg. 40)	2-3	10-12	10-12
Shoulders			
1. Behind neck press (pg. 29)	2-3	10-12	10
2. Bent lateral raises (pg. 40)	2-3	10-12	10
Back			
1. Lat pull down (pg. 30)	2-3	10-12	10-15
2. Bent-over row (pg. 41)	2-3	10-12	10-15
Arms			
1. Standing dumbbell curls (pg. 42)	2-3	10-12	5-10
2. Dumbbell kickbacks (pg. 42)	2-3	10-12	3-5
Legs			
1. Squat (pg. 33)	2-3	10-12	10-15
2. Leg extensions (pg. 43)	2-3	10-12	10-15
3. Standing calf raises (pg. 44)	3-4	10-15	10-15
Cool-down (pg. 16)	5-10 minutes		

REAR LEG SWING

Rear leg swings are excellent for trimming your hips and waist, as well as working your buttocks and legs. Start on your hands and knees. Extend your right leg to the side, keeping it straight and at a ninety-degree angle to your body; look at your right foot (Photo 62). Now swing your right leg back, over to the left, and turn your head to the left, looking at your foot (Photo 63). Do all of this in the same movement. Swing the right leg back to your starting position, and continue to do all repetitions without pause; alternate with your left leg. Keep your leg straight and as high as possible as you swing it!

Photo 62

Photo 63

INCLINE FLYS

This will firm and strengthen your chest muscles, especially in the upper chest. It is also excellent for giving your bustline a lift! Lie on your back on an inclined bench (approximately a 45-degree incline). Hold a light dumbbell in each hand directly over your chest, with the wrists facing each other (Photo 64). Slowly lower the dumbbells out to the sides and down, keeping palms up, as far as you can comfortably (Photo 65). Then, using your chest muscles, slowly pull the weights back to starting position and repeat.

Two sets of ten reps each will be challenging at the start; work to the point where you can finish three sets of twelve reps each. It is very important in this movement to keep your elbows slightly bent throughout, to avoid straining them. This exercise can be done on either a flat or inclined bench, depending on the area of the chest you want to develop.

Photo 64   Photo 65

BENT LATERAL RAISE

This movement will help to shape your shoulders, and also works the upper back. Begin by standing with your feet about shoulder width apart and your knees slightly bent. Holding a light dumbbell in each hand, bend slightly forward at the waist, letting your arms hang (Photo 66). Now slowly raise the dumbbells up and out (while keeping palms level at all times) to just above shoulder level (Photo 67). Slowly lower the weights back to the starting position and repeat.

Bent lateral raises should initially be done in two sets of ten reps. Gradually increase this to three sets of twelve reps. Elbows stay slightly bent throughout this exercise to avoid injury; be sure to raise and lower the weights slowly and smoothly.

Photo 66

Photo 67

BENT-OVER ROWING

This exercise works the upper back and arms. Stand with your feet comfortably apart and grasp a light barbell with an overhand grip, slightly wider than shoulder width. Bend forward at the waist, until upper body is parallel to the floor. Let your arms hang straight. Keep knees slightly bent and back straight (Photo 68). Now pull the barbell up to your chest, keeping back still and elbows up (Photo 69). Slowly lower the bar back to starting position.

Start out with two sets of ten reps each; build up to three

sets of a dozen reps apiece. The key is to keep your back flat at all times to avoid injury.

STANDING DUMBBELL CURLS (ALTERNATING)

This exercise will help strengthen your upper arms. Start with your feet comfortably apart and keep your back straight. Hold a light dumbbell in each hand, using an underhand grip. With your arms and wrists straight, extend them downward so they are resting across your upper thighs (Photo 70). Keep your elbow in close to your body and slowly curl one of the dumbbells upward toward your shoulder and pause (Photo 71). Slowly lower the dumbbell back to starting position. Repeat with the other arm and continue alternating until you reach your desired number of repetitions.

Begin with two sets of ten reps each; and progress to three sets of twelve reps. Be sure to keep your elbow in tight to your body; only move your forearms when curling the weight upward.

DUMBBELL KICKBACKS

This exercise will help develop your triceps, the muscles at the back of the upper arms, and also will work the rear of your shoulders. Begin by standing with your feet comfortably

Photo 68   Photo 69

apart; bend forward at the waist. While holding a light dumb-bell in each hand, place your elbows close to your sides, bent at a right angle. Keep your upper arms parallel to the floor at all times (Photo 72). Slowly push forearms up and back until your arms are fully extended, and pause (Photo 73). Slowly lower dumbbells back to starting position and repeat.

Two sets of ten reps should be gradually extended to three sets of twelve reps. It is crucial to this movement to keep your upper arms pulled in tight to your body and to control the weights at all times.

Photo 70   Photo 71

LEG EXTENSION

Leg extensions are good for toning and shaping the front thigh muscles, especially around the knee area. Sit at the end of leg extension machine and hold the sides of the machine to brace yourself. Hook your feet under the lower set of rollers (Photo 74). Using good control and a smooth steady motion, slowly raise your legs up until they are fully extended and pause (Photo 75). Now, slowly lower the weight back to starting position and repeat.

Again, two sets of ten are fine at the beginning; work up to three sets of twelve reps. It's also important that you con-centrate and do each repetition slowly, without jerking the weight.

Photo 72

Photo 73

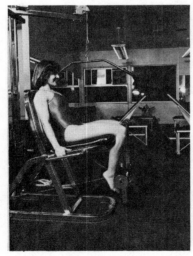

Photo 74

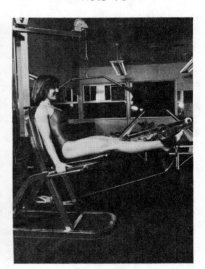

Photo 75

STANDING CALF RAISES

This exercise will improve your entire calf, from ankle to knee! To begin, position yourself comfortably under the calf machine, with feet about six inches apart and toes pointed

INTERMEDIATE PROGRESS CHART

STARTING	1st WEEK	2nd WEEK	3rd WEEK	4th WEEK	5th WEEK	6th WEEK	7th WEEK	8th WEEK	LOSS
BODY WEIGHT									
BUSTLINE									
WAISTLINE									
HIPS									
THIGHS									
CALVES									
UPPER ARMS									

straight forward on calf block. Let your heels stretch down as low as possible, keeping legs straight (Photo 76). Now push yourself up (without jerking) on your toes, as high as you can (Photo 77). Slowly, lower yourself down as you return to starting position; repeat. Start with three sets of ten reps each, and work up to four sets of fifteen.

To get the full benefit from this movement, it is very important to stretch all the way down, pause, then raise up on the toes as high as possible, and pause.

Photo 76

Photo 77

5

Advanced Program

At this point you should have experienced exciting changes in your body, and may have the desire to try an advanced training program. Before you start an advanced program like the one outlined here, you should have at least four to six months of training experience as a foundation. The following four-day advanced routine is designed to teach you new movements, increase your endurance, as well as firm and shape your entire body.

Concentration is the key factor in advanced training. You must be in full control of your thoughts, keep them free from daily distractions, and apply them totally to your training. Be sure to concentrate on the muscle group being worked and try to relax your other body parts.

Remember, only you can provide the motivation and determination necessary to make your weight training program successful and enjoyable. You can then experience how it feels to have a firm, healthy body and the self-confidence that it brings with it. It will then become a vital part of your life!

HANGING KNEE-UP

This is an excellent exercise for working the lower abdominal muscles. Begin by hanging from a high horizontal bar with your feet off the floor, and using a wide overhand grip (Photo 78). Slowly pull your knees up toward your chest, keeping legs together (Photo 79). Lower your legs down, returning to starting position, and repeat.

To start, aim for three sets of ten reps, four sets of fifteen should be the goal. It's important for you to control your body throughout this movement and try not to let it swing back and forth.

Photo 78   Photo 79

BENT LEG SIT-UPS

This is a terrific stomach exercise, especially for tightening and strengthening your upper abdomen. Start out by placing your feet under foot straps on a sit-up board, and bend legs at a right angle. Cross hands on chest and start with upper body curled up to knees (Photo 80). Now slowly lower your upper body to an extended position (Photo 81). Then return to starting position and repeat.

Three sets of fifteen reps each should steadily be increased to four sets of twenty-five. Be sure to use a smooth, continuous motion throughout this exercise. For added resistance, move the board up. The steeper the incline, the more difficult this becomes. You can also increase the number of repetitions.

ADVANCED PROGRAM
(Monday and Thursday)

Exercises

Warm-ups (pg. 7)	5 - 10 minutes	
Stretching (pg. 10)	5 - 10 minutes	

	Sets	Reps	Weight
Stomach			
1. Hanging knee-up (pg. 47)	3-4	10-15	0
2. Bent leg sit-ups (pg. 48)	3-4	15-25	0
Hips and Waist			
1. Dumbbell side bends (pg. 49)	2	10-15	3-5
2. Seated twist (pg. 50)	2	25-50	0
Legs			
1. Leg press (pg. 52)	3-4	10-15	10-20
2. Leg lunges (pg. 53)	3-4	10-15	5-10
3. Leg curls (pg. 54)	3-4	10-15	10-20
Back			
1. Good morning (pg. 54)	2-3	10-15	10-15
2. Lat pull down (pg. 30)	2-3	10-15	10-20
3. Hyperextensions (pg. 55)	2-3	10-15	0
Calves			
1. Standing calf raises (pg. 44)	2-3	12-15	10-20
2. Seated calf raises (pg. 57)	2-3	12-15	10-20
Cool-down (pg. 16)	5-10 minutes		

DUMBBELL SIDE BENDS

This exercise works the oblique muscles at the sides of your waist, and will help tone and slim your entire waist area. Stand with your feet shoulder width apart; holding a light dumbbell in each hand, and arms hanging straight down at your sides (Photo 82), bend slowly down to one side as far as possible and pause (Photo 83); return to starting position. Then bend to the other side as far as possible. Continue alternating.

Two sets of ten to fifteen reps each are sufficient for this exercise. Be sure to use light weights and high repetitions, because you don't want to build the obliques.

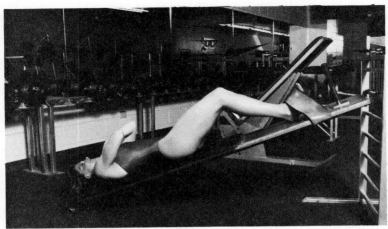

Photo 80

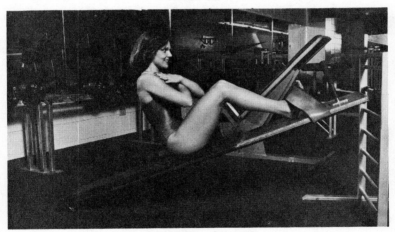

Photo 81

SEATED TWIST

This movement will help trim your waistline and upper hips, and will also increase upper body flexibility. Sitting on the end of a flat bench, place a light bar across your shoulders, and wrap your arms around it. Remember to keep your back straight (Photo 84). Slowly twist your upper body as far to the left as possible (Photo 85), and then to the right, in a continuous motion.

Start with two sets of twenty-five reps each, and work up to fifty repetitions. This is a light weight, high repetition exercise, mainly for reducing. Increase your reps, not the amount of weight. Heavy weights can build the oblique muscles on your sides, making your waist appear wider.

Photo 82

Photo 83

Photo 84

Photo 85

LEG PRESS

This is another good exercise for working your legs, especially the upper thighs. Begin by placing your feet on the machine about a foot apart, with legs fully extended (Photo 86). Lower the weight down slowly, as far as you can, to get a good stretch (Photo 87). Now slowly press forward, returning to starting position, and repeat.

Three sets of ten reps each for starters; increase this to four sets of fifteen as you progress. Do not allow the weight to drop; lower it slowly and be sure you are in complete control of the weight at all times.

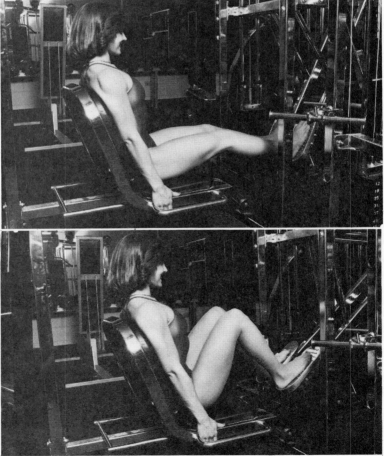

Photo 86, top; Photo 87, bottom

LEG LUNGES

This exercise will strengthen and tone the thighs, and will help to firm and lift your buttocks. Stand with your feet fairly close together and place a light barbell across your shoulders, gripping bar (Photo 88). Then take a big step forward, and lower into a lunge position, while keeping back straight (Photo 89). Push yourself back to the starting position and repeat with your other leg and continue. Ten reps done in three sets is enough for openers; build up to four sets of fifteen apiece.

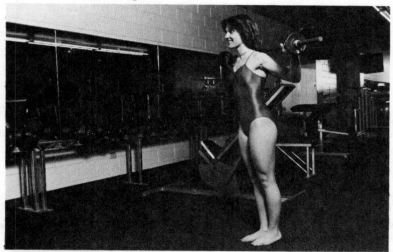

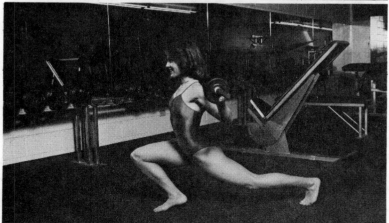

Photo 88, top; Photo 89, bottom

LEG CURL

The leg curl is the best exercise for directly working the back of your thighs. Begin by lying face down on leg curl bench with your heels hooked under pads, holding the sides of bench to help support your upper body (Photo 90). Slowly curl the weight upward toward buttock as far as possible, and pause momentarily (Photo 91). Return to starting position and repeat.

Three sets of ten reps each at the start; work up to four sets of fifteen. You want the back of your legs to pull the weight up, so be sure to keep your hips down on the bench throughout the exercise.

GOOD MORNING

This is an excellent exercise for your lower back, giving the back better support and helping to improve posture.

To begin, place a very light barbell across your shoulders, using a wide overhand grip. Your feet are about shoulder width apart and knees are slightly bent (Photo 92). Begin leaning forward until your upper body is parallel to the floor (Photo 93). Now, keeping your back straight, rise up to starting position and continue.

Two sets of ten reps each should be built up to three sets of fifteen. Remember to keep your stomach pulled in. Also, hyperextensions are a good substitute for this exercise.

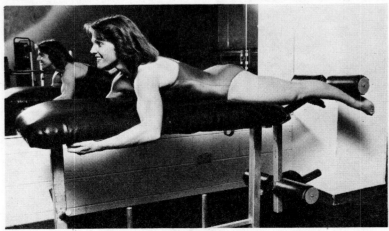

Photo 90

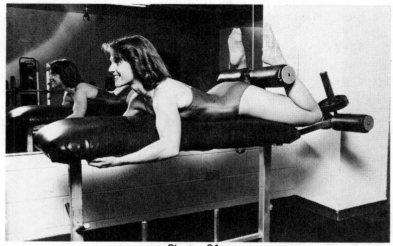

Photo 91

Photo 92

Photo 93

HYPEREXTENSIONS

Hyperextensions are one of the best exercises known for the lower back muscles. Begin by lying face down on hyperextension bench with ankles under the pads. Place your hands behind your head and keep upper body parallel to floor

(Photo 94). Then, very slowly lower upper body to a vertical position (Photo 95). Now raise back up to starting position and repeat.

This exercise is very intense, so start by only doing a few reps at a time, and gradually work up; aim for three sets of fifteen reps. This can also be done on a high bench with someone holding your feet down.

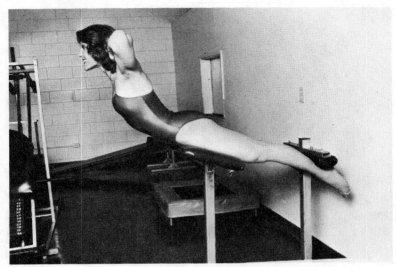

Photo 94

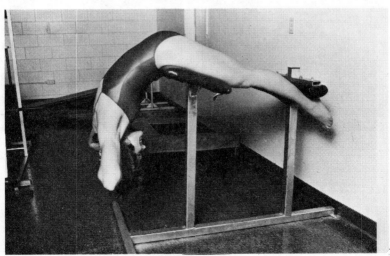

Photo 95

SEATED CALF RAISES

This exercise will help to firm and shape your entire calf area. Sit at the calf machine, resting the pads on your knees, and place toes about eight inches apart and facing forward. Now, let your heels drop down as far as possible and pause (Photo 96). Slowly rise up on your toes as high as possible and pause (Photo 97). Lower back to starting position and repeat.

Start with a dozen seated calf raises, and do two sets; work up to three sets of fifteen. If you want to work the outside part of the calf, point your toes in. To work the inside, point toes out and rise up and down on them. Do these movements slowly, using control.

CABLE PULLS

This is a very effective chest exercise. Stand with your feet fairly wide apart for balance and keep your back straight. Grasp the cable handle in one hand and extend arm out to side (Photo 98). Using your chest muscles, pull the cable across your upper body in a controlled manner (Photo 99). Slowly return to fully extended position. Repeat and complete desired number of reps, then alternate with the other arm.

Photo 96

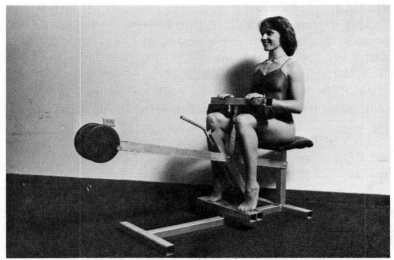

Photo 97

Photo 98

Photo 99

Do three sets of ten for openers; increase steadily to four sets of fifteen. This movement can be done standing straight as shown, or bending slightly forward to change the angle, whichever way you prefer.

ADVANCED PROGRAM
(Tuesday and Friday)

Exercises

Warm-ups (pg. 7)	5 - 10 minutes
Stretching (pg. 10)	5 - 10 minutes

	Sets	Reps	Weight
Stomach			
1. Leg raises (pg. 36)	3-4	15-25	0
2. Bent leg sit-ups (pg. 48)	3-4	15-25	0
Hips and Waist			
1. Seated twist (pg. 50)	2	50-75	0
2. Rear leg swing (pg. 38)	2	15-25	0
Chest			
1. Incline flys (pg. 40)	3-4	10-15	10-15
2. Cable pulls (pg. 57)	3-4	10-15	10-15
3. Incline barbell press (pg. 59)	3-4	10-15	10-15
Shoulders			
1. Behind neck press (pg. 29)	2-3	10-15	10-15
2. Upright row (pg. 60)	2-3	10-15	10-15
Arms			
1. Incline dumbbell curls (pg. 61)	2-3	10-15	5-10
2. Tricep pushdown (pg. 61)	2-3	10-15	10-15
3. Wrist curls (reverse) (pg. 63)	1-2	10-15	5-10
Cool-down (pg. 16)	5-10 minutes		

INCLINE BARBELL PRESS

This exercise is a great way to develop your upper pectorals or chest muscles. Shoulders and arms will also benefit.

Lie back on an incline bench and grasp a light barbell with a slightly wider than shoulder grip, and place barbell at straight arms length, above your chest (Photo 100). Then slowly move barbell straight down until it touches your mid-chest (Photo 101). Press barbell upward, returning to starting position and repeat. Work on three sets of ten to begin, and aim for four sets of fifteen reps each. A 45-degree incline is best for working the upper chest.

UPRIGHT ROW

This exercise will shape your shoulders and arms. Begin with your hands about six inches apart, using a light barbell with an overhand grip. Your arms should be fully extended in front of your thighs and feet comfortably apart (Photo 102). Pull the weight up under your chin, keeping your elbow high (Photo 103). Slowly return to starting position and repeat.

Start with two sets of ten reps, increase this to three sets of fifteen. Remember, good form is more important than the amount of weight you use.

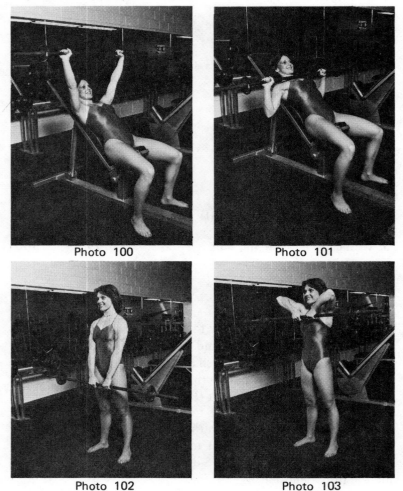

Photo 100   Photo 101

Photo 102   Photo 103

INCLINE DUMBBELL CURLS

This exercise will help you to strengthen your upper arms; it will work the biceps from a new angle. To begin, lie on inclined bench at about a 45 degree angle with your arms hanging at your sides, holding a light dumbbell in each hand (Photo 104). Curl the dumbbells slowly, while keeping the palms up and elbows at your sides, to your upper chest area (Photo 105). Lower dumbbells back to starting position.

Ten reps at the start, and work to be able to do fifteen. Move from two to three sets. It's important to keep palms level throughout the movement, and remember to keep your elbows at your sides.

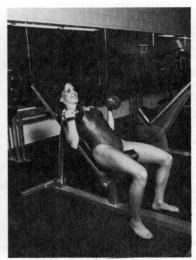

Photo 104   Photo 105

TRICEP PUSHDOWN

This exercise will strengthen, shape, and firm the back of your upper arms. With a narrow overhand grip on the lat bar, begin with arms bent and close to your sides, with the bar even with your chest (Photo 106). Keeping elbows pinned to your sides, push the bar down and outward, moving only your forearms (Photo 107). Slowly bring the bar up as you return to your starting position.

The key to this movement is to keep the elbows tight into

ADVANCED PROGRESS CHART

STARTING	1st WEEK	2nd WEEK	3rd WEEK	4th WEEK	5th WEEK	6th WEEK	7th WEEK	8th WEEK	LOSS
BODY WEIGHT									
BUSTLINE									
WAISTLINE									
HIPS									
THIGHS									
CALVES									
UPPER ARMS									

your sides and your back straight; don't move anything except your forearms in this exercise. Start with two sets of ten and build up to three sets of fifteen.

WRIST CURLS

This will tone your forearm muscles. Sit on the end of a bench with light dumbbells, using an overhand grip and your hands about four inches apart. Rest forearms on your thighs,

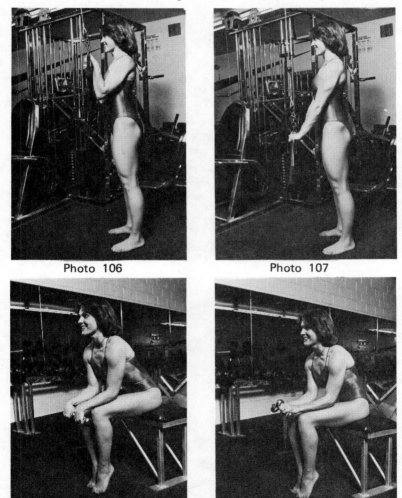

Photo 106   Photo 107

Photo 108   Photo 109

and (with wrists extended beyond the knees) flex hands downward as far as possible (Photo 108). From this position, curl the weight up as high as possible and pause (Photo 109). Slowly lower to starting position and repeat.

Just do one set of ten for openers. Work gradually up to two sets of fifteen reps. This is a high rep, light weight movement. Be sure to use a slow, steady motion, letting your forearms do all the work.

6

Diet and Nutrition

Proper nutrition may be defined as the ingestion of the six basic nutrients in proper amounts and proportions to ensure health. These nutrients are protein, carbohydrates, fats, vitamins, minerals, and water, and the key to good health is to maintain an adequate daily intake of all of them.

Anyone who takes up weight training should have a basic understanding of nutrition. An exercise program by itself is not enough. Exercise will tone existing muscles, but to go further, you must have all the nutrients needed to promote well-being. This can only be accomplished by good eating habits.

Exercise is only half of the battle. Proper diet and nutrition is the other half, and together these two will enable you to achieve your goal of ultimate health. In this chapter I will cover some basic information on these nutrients and their functions in promoting good health. I hope that these explanations will clear up much of the confusion on the subject of nutrition. So much has been written about this subject that it is no wonder that many people are confused.

There are three basic nutrients needed to maintain good health. They are protein, carbohydrates, and fats. Proteins are the most important nutrient for they are the materials for growth and maintenance of every cell and muscle tissue. There has been much confusion about the amount of protein needed daily. A simple formula to figure out your amount of protein is to figure one gram of protein for every pound of body weight.

The best source of protein is complete protein which can be obtained from eggs, fish, poultry, meat, and dairy products. Your need for protein does not change when dieting. Weight control is accomplished by increasing or reducing the total calorie intake per day from fats and carbohydrates, but your daily intake of protein should remain the same.

Carbohydrates are made up of sugars and starches; these supply the body with the energy you need for physical activity. Carbohydrates also aid in the utilization of protein in the growth and repair of muscle tissue. It is very important that you get your carbohydrates from natural sources and not refined or processed foods such as white sugar, refined breads, bakery products of all kinds, or soft drinks. The best sources of carbohydrates are fruits, vegetables, and whole grains.

Fats are the third basic nutrient; their primary function, like carbohydrates, is to supply energy, but at a much slower rate. Fats take almost twice as long to burn as carbohydrates, so carbohydrates are a much more efficient nutrient. A certain amount of fats is essential to good health, as they provide a necessary base for carrying vitamins A, D, E, F, and K.

Now that you have become familiar with the three crucial nutrients, the next most important nutrients are vitamins and minerals. Together with proteins, carbohydrates, fats, and water, they cannot be eliminated from our diet without causing great harm to our bodies. Vitamins and minerals act as catalysts with other nutrients to maintain a healthy body. There are two types of vitamins; one is water-soluble, like the B and C complexes, which must be replaced every day and are measured in milligrams. The others are the fat-soluble vitamins, like A, D, and E, that can be stored in the body and are measured in I.U.'s (international units).

In the following pages, I have listed the vitamins and minerals that your body needs for proper health. Each listing is accompanied by important facts and advice so that it is easily understood and applied.

VITAMIN A

Vitamin A is a fat-soluble vitamin that is stored in your liver and kidneys. It is important for maintaining healthy hair, nails, and skin, and is also crucial to normal growth and bone development. Also affected by Vitamin A are digestion, reproduction, your tooth enamel and the cholesterol level in the blood.

Best Food Sources:

liver	broccoli
cheese	sunflower seeds
corn	tomatoes
egg yolk	peas

Symptoms of Deficiency:

1. Sensitivity to bright light
2. Skin dryness and roughness
3. Fingernails break and peel easily
4. Dandruff accumulates

VITAMIN B-COMPLEX

Vitamin B is a water-soluble vitamin and cannot be stored in the body, so it must be replaced every day. There are at least fifteen members of the B-Complex family and it is essential that all are present because they work together to be most effective.

The group of substances in this family promotes good health in many ways. They are important for normal digestion, calm nerves, a healthy liver, and improving the skin, arteries, and eyes.

Best Food Sources:

liver	fowl
kidneys	fish
cheese	yogurt
egg yolk	whole grains

Symptoms of Deficiency:

1. Nervousness
2. Fatigue

3. Constipation
4. Shortness of breath
5. Insomnia
6. Headaches
7. Depression

VITAMIN C-COMPLEX

Vitamin C-Complex, like Vitamin B-Complex, is water-soluble, essential for health, and most beneficial when all components of the complex are present in the body.

Vitamin C is important for the elasticity and strength of cells and connective tissue. It also aids in maintaining the body's resistance to infection, colds, and cuts, and is needed for healthy teeth and bones. Another great benefit is Vitamin C's action as a detoxifier of chemicals within the body such as food additives, dyes, and chemical components of air pollution. Smokers must supplement their diet with Vitamin C-Complex because the greatest single destroyer of this vitamin is regular smoking. One cigarette will neutralize about twenty-five milligrams of Vitamin C, which is 500 mg. per pack.

Best Food Sources:

citrus fruits	peas
cantaloupe	potatoes
tomatoes	liver
green vegetables	corn

Symptoms of Deficiency:

1. Aching bones, joints, and muscles
2. Fatigue
3. Colds
4. Worsening of allergies
5. Shortness of breath

VITAMIN D

Vitamin D is another fat-soluble vitamin that is especially needed by children. It is required for proper utilization of calcium and phosphorous in the body, which promotes healthy teeth and bones. Vitamin D is produced by the action of sunlight on a substance secreted by the oil glands of the skin, thus earning the nickname, the "sunshine vitamin".

Best Food Sources:

liver
milk
eggs
fish
oysters

Symptoms of Deficiency:

1. Fatigue
2. Arthritis
3. Nervous tension

VITAMIN E

Vitamin E is a fat-soluble vitamin that is truly unique. It is essential for healthy functioning of the cardiovascular system, which is obviously needed by everyone, especially athletes.

One of the most important effects of Vitamin E is oxygen conservation. By keeping your oxygen supply up, Vitamin E makes it easier for the body to function normally, and build up a reserve for future needs. This becomes even more important for physically active people. Vitamin E also dilates the blood vessels and prevents clots from forming in the veins, arteries, and capillaries. In addition this vitamin is an aid in the healing of bruises, burns, and scar tissue, and is very important for normal functioning of the sex glands.

Best Food Sources:

wheat germ	sunflower seeds
whole grains	olive oil
liver	peanut oil
eggs	rice (brown)
avocados	kelp

Symptoms of Deficiency

1. Varicose veins
2. Headaches
3. Menopause distress
4. Painful breasts

5. Acne
6. Asthma
7. Heart ailments

VITAMIN F

Vitamin F, or unsaturated fatty acids, are important for healthy skin, calm nerves, and the absorption of all the fat-soluble vitamins. Other benefits from vitamin F are the lowering of cholesterol in the blood and better distribution of calcium to the tissues.

Best Food Sources;

corn oil	whole grains
cotton seed oil	peanuts
safflower oil	sunflower seeds

VITAMIN K

Vitamin K is produced in the intestinal tract and is a blood clotting element; it helps stop hemorrhaging due to injury, surgery, childbirth, or other bodily traumas. It also helps in the normal functioning of the liver.

Best Food Sources:

leafy green vegetables
kelp
milk

VITAMIN P

Vitamin P (bioflavinoids) are water-soluble and are always accompanied by Vitamin C. For this reason, if you buy Vitamin C, always get 100% natural Vitamin C-Complex, not ascorbic acid. Vitamin P promotes healthy capillaries and helps build the body's basic resistance to infections.

Best Food Sources:

citrus fruits
grapes
rose hips
green peppers

CALCIUM

Calcium, the most abundant mineral in your body, is considered the most important. Every muscle in your body relies on calcium for its normal functioning. This mineral comprises more than two percent of your body weight; virtually all of this calcium is stored in your bones and teeth. The mineral is also essential for normal muscle contraction and nerve function, and is used as a natural pain reliever and tranquilizer.

Best Food Sources:

fish	whole grains
cheese	yogurt
eggs	fruits, fresh
poultry	non-pasteurized milk

CHLORINE

Chlorine is essential for the production of hydrochloric acid, which is important for good digestion and helps regulate the body's acid/alkali balance.

Best Food Sources:

table salt
rare meat
beets
leafy greens
ripe olives

CHROMIUM

Chromium is a mineral which is of particular importance in metabolizing and transporting glucose to the cells, where it is used for energy.

Best Food Sources:

meats
brewer's yeast
whole grains
liver

COBALT

Cobalt is essential for the normal operation and maintenance of cells. An adequate supply of cobalt promotes healthy red blood and will fend off anemia.

Best Food Sources:

liver
clams
oysters
milk

COPPER

Copper aids in the utilization of Vitamin C and is necessary for the proper use of iron by the body. Copper is also important for the production of red blood cells, normal nerve functioning, and preserving hair color.

Best Food Sources:

liver	leafy green vegetables
eggs	almonds
shrimp	clams

IODINE

Iodine is a trace mineral that is vital to the proper functioning of the thyroid gland. Because of its action upon the thyroid, it indirectly affects metabolism, the nerves, and endurance.

Best Food Sources:

fish	garlic
kelp	mushrooms
shellfish	milk products

IRON

Iron is important in the building of healthy red blood cells, which prevents anemia, and also promotes normal blood sugar level. Iron is needed to carry a supply of oxygen through the body to the billions of individual cells.

Best Food Sources:

liver	oysters
turkey	beef
egg yolk	clams
green vegetables	

MAGNESIUM

Magnesium is another mineral that is important for normal muscular function. It is also essential for good bone development and aids in carbohydrate metabolism.

Best Food Sources:

almonds	walnuts
wheat germ	peanuts
kelp	pecans
green vegetables	

MANGANESE

Manganese is an important catalyst in the utilization of the B and C vitamins, and also helps to promote normal bone growth.

Best Food Sources:

eggs
whole grains
green vegetables
oranges

PHOSPHOROUS

Phosphorous takes part in chemical reactions with proteins, fats, and carbohydrates to play a role in virtually all of the body's functions. This mineral combines with calcium to create strong bones and aids in maintaining the body's acid/alkaline balance.

Best Food Sources:

meat	eggs
fish	nuts
cheese	whole grains
poultry	soy beans

POTASSIUM

This mineral is as vital to the heart and nerves as calcium is to the bones. Potassium combines with phosphorous to help transport oxygen to the entire muscular system, and aids in the utilization of protein.

Best Food Sources:

whole grains
kelp
fruits
green vegetables
potatoes

SELENIUM

Selenium is an essential trace mineral that acts as an anti-toxin. Also, it is an important agent for promoting growth, and helps prevent aging.

Best Food Sources:

bran
eggs
kelp
milk

SODIUM

Sodium is another mineral which is vital to balance the acid/alkaline content in the blood. Sodium, in conjunction with potassium, aids in muscle activity and maintains normal water balance in the body.

Best Food Sources:

table salt
sea food
poultry
carrots
meat

SULPHUR

Sulphur is an important mineral for maintaining healthy hair, nails, and skin. This mineral helps in the metabolism of carbohydrates and the reproduction of healthy tissues.

Best Food Sources:

eggs
brussel sprouts
mustard greens
almonds

ZINC

Zinc is a mineral which is present in all tissues. It produces several enzymes which aid in proper digestion and metabolism. Zinc also is important for growth and normal development of the reproductive glands.

Best Food Sources:

wheat germ
eggs
oysters
green leafy vegetables
sunflower seeds

7

Weight Control

Many women embark upon an exercise program to lose, gain, or simply maintain their weight. Exercise alone is not really sufficient to control weight. The best and quickest way to produce results is to combine exercise with proper nutrition. Quick weight reduction or gain is not either practical or sensible. It is in fact dangerous and can cause many difficulties with your health.

The word "diet" is very often misunderstood. Many people hear the word and automatically think only of losing weight. Diet rather is a word that describes your eating habits; which means you can be dieting to gain, lose, or maintain your body weight.

The simplest and best way to control your weight is by watching the total number of calories taken daily. If you take in more calories than your body can use, it will convert and store the excess as fat; if you consume fewer calories than your body burns up, you will lose weight. Weight control is actually that simple, but what is not always so simple is to obtain these calories from the proper foods. To eat properly you should choose from the four basic food groups and try to include these in your daily diet.

Of course, whenever possible the source of these calories should be from foods free of chemical additives; try to avoid freezing or over-cooking, as this will deplete food of vital

FOUR BASIC GROUPS

Dairy Products

a. Yogurt
b. Cheese
c. Milk

Protein

a. Fish
b. Poultry
c. Meat

Fruits and Vegetables

Grains

a. Breads
b. Cereals

vitamins, enzymes, and minerals. The recommended proportions of the basic food elements from which you should try to obtain your calories are: 50% natural carbohydrates, 30% complete protein, and 20% from fats.

Now that you have a basic understanding of nutrition, you can apply it to your own eating patterns to help control your weight. The need for protein always remains constant. But you can adjust your intake of carbohydrates and fats to maintain a caloric total that will best suit your goals.

The most effective and sensible way to gain or lose weight is to adjust your calorie intake so that you will gain or lose no more than one pound per week. To do this, simply increase or decrease your daily intake by 500 calories. This will add up to 3500 calories per week, which is equal to one pound. You can buy a calorie counter book at your local drug store that will supply you with information on the number of calories in almost all basic food items. Use this book to monitor your daily calorie intake. Apply the calorie chart and sample diets in this chapter to suit your individual needs.

On the following pages are three basic diets that I use to help maintain, lose, or gain weight. I never let my body weight fluctuate more than five pounds either way, which I feel is best for good health. These are only sample diets; you should adjust your food intake to your own needs. As you can see in these diets, the total amount of food consumed daily remains about the same in all three. What *does* change are the types of food consumed. For example, if you want to lose weight, you would eat chicken or fish to meet your protein requirements instead of beef, because they are lower in calories. The same is true with fruits; strawberries and cantaloupes are low in calories, compared to apples and oranges, but you can still eat fruit.

So you can see that what is important here is to choose the right foods. By using a calorie counter you will soon learn how many calories different foods contain, and you will be able to choose the proper foods for your diet.

SAMPLE DIET TO MAINTAIN BODY WEIGHT

Desired weight: 110   Approx: 2200 Calories
Daily allowance: Approx: 2200 Calories

Breakfast

2 eggs any style
3-4 ounces meat (hamburger, bacon, or ham)
1 slice whole grain toast with butter
Fruit (low calorie such as strawberries or cantaloupe)
Coffee or tea (if sweetened, use honey)

Lunch

Turkey sandwich on whole wheat bread
Small green salad with low-cal dressing
Fruit (orange, apple)
Coffee, tea, or diet soda

Dinner

Large portion of chicken, fish, or beef
Green vegetables (broccoli or asparagus)
Dinner salad
Coffee, tea, or low-cal dressing
Yogurt, cheese, or real ice cream

SAMPLE DIET FOR LOSING WEIGHT

Desired weight: 105   subtract 500 calories
Normal weight: 110   2200 calories
Daily allowance: 1700 calories
Approx. five weeks to reach desired weight

Breakfast

2 eggs any style
2 slices whole grain toast with butter
fruit, any low-calorie
coffee or tea

Lunch

Large salad—tuna, chicken, crab, or shrimp
Low calorie dressing
1 roll with butter
fruit, any low-calorie
coffee, tea, or low-cal beverage

Dinner

Medium portion of chicken or fish (no meat)
Green vegetables
Small dinner salad
Low calorie fruit or yogurt
Coffee or tea

Best snacks: Celery, popcorn (no butter), low-calorie fruit such as strawberries or cantaloupe.

SAMPLE DIET FOR GAINING WEIGHT

Desired weight: 115   Add 500 calories
Normal weight: 110   2200 calories
Daily allowance: Approx. 2700 calories

Breakfast

2 eggs any style
Meat (3-4 ounces)
2 slices whole grain toast with butter
Juice (4-6 ounces)
coffee or tea

Lunch

Sandwich (any type meat) on whole wheat
Small green salad
Fruit (orange, apple, any high-cal fruit)
Coffee, tea, milk (6 ounces)

Dinner

Large portion of meat
Yellow vegetable (squash, corn, etc.)
Dinner salad
Coffee, tea, or low-cal beverage

Best Snacks: Protein drink containing juice (apple, orange, etc.) approx. 8 ounces, 1 raw egg, 2 tablespoons (milk and egg) protein powder, blended all together with ice.

CALORIE CHART

Calorie Allowances for Women (To Maintain Body Weight)

DESIRED WEIGHT (lbs.)	NORMAL (active)	WEIGHT TRAINER
95	1520	1900
98	1568	1960
101	1616	2020
105	1680	2100
110	1760	2200
115	1840	2300
120	1920	2400
125	2000	2500
130	2080	2600
135	2160	2700
140	2240	2800
145	2320	2900
150	2400	3000
155	2480	3100
160	2560	3200
165	2640	3300
175	2800	3500
185	2960	3700
195	3120	3900
200	3200	4000

8

Training for Specific Sports

In this chapter I will cover specific exercises that best complement various sports in which you may be active. Before starting any of these training programs, you should have at least gone through the beginner's course in this book.

The training programs outlined in this chapter should be added to your regular program during the off-season of your sport. During the season, when you are active in your sport, you should reduce your training to a maintenance program. By this I mean two workouts per week on days when you are not participating in your sport.

These training programs are only a guideline. You are your own best coach and must be honest with yourself; look for your weak areas that need developing. By applying good nutrition and training to improve these weak areas, as well as overall strength, you will find that your level of performance will steadily increase. Many athletes today are using various weight training methods to increase performance, not only in sports like football and wrestling, but golf and tennis as well. Weight training enhances these activities by increasing endurance, strength, and flexibility.

Top athletes will attest to the benefits of weight lifting, such as Brian Oldfield (track and field), O. J. Simpson (football), Karl Swartz (skier), Billie Jean King (tennis), and even Bobby Fischer (chess). You too can realize your full potential and benefit greatly from weight training.

GYMNASTICS

Muscles Needing Development:

A. Stomach
B. Back
C. Shoulders
D. Triceps

Exercises	Sets	Reps
A. Stomach (leg raises, pg. 36)	3-4	20-25
B. Stomach (bent leg sit-ups, pg. 48)	3-4	20-25
C. Back (lat pull-downs, pg. 30)	3-4	8-10
D. Shoulders (behind neck press, pg. 29)	3-4	10-12
E. Triceps (tricep push-down, pg. 61)	2-3	10-12

These exercises will greatly improve your strength in most movements for gymnastics, but here the athlete is her own best coach. You will have to decide what areas you are weak in and concentrate on them to suit your needs.

SWIMMING

Muscles Needing Development:

A. Back
B. Lower back
C. Shoulders
D. Thighs
E. Stomach

Exercises	Sets	Reps
A. Back (lat pull-down, pg. 30)	3-4	10-12
B. Back (bent-over rows, pg. 41)	3-4	10-12
C. Lower back (hyperextensions, pg. 55)	2-3	8-10
D. Shoulders (bent lateral raises, pg. 40)	3-4	10-12
E. Thighs (extensions, pg. 43)	3-4	10-12
F. Stomach (bent knee sit-ups, pg. 48)	3-4	20-25

The most important areas to develop in this group are the back and shoulder muscles. You should focus intently on these during the off-season. The East Germans have had great success in swimming with help from their extensive weight training programs.

SKIING (SNOW)

Muscles Needing Development:

A. Thighs
B. Stomach
C. Calves
D. Shoulders

Exercises	Sets	Reps
A. Thighs (squats, pg. 33)	3-4	8-10
B. Thighs (leg extensions, pg. 43)	3-4	10-12
C. Stomach (side bends, pg. 49)	3-4	20-25
D. Calves (seated calf raises, pg. 57)	3-4	15-20
E. Shoulders (dumbbell flys, pg. 40)	3-4	10-12

As you can see, this program is mostly designed for leg development, which is the most important area for skiing. Another key factor is endurance. This can be greatly improved by high reps of hindu-jumps (pg. 133).

BASKETBALL AND VOLLEYBALL

Muscles Needing Development:

A. Thighs
B. Calves

Exercises	Sets	Reps
A. Thighs (leg extensions, pg, 43)	3-4	10-20
B. Thighs (hindu-jumps, pg. 133)	3-4	20
C. Calves (standing calf raises, pg. 45)	3-4	15

Include these exercises in your regular program and train at a faster pace than normal to help build endurance. Drop back to two workouts per week during the regular season.

CYCLING

Muscles Needing Development:

A. Thighs
B. Calves
C. Lower back
D. Hamstrings

Exercises	Sets	Reps
A. Thighs (leg extensions, pg. 43)	3-4	12-15

B. Calves (seated calf raises, pg. 57)	3-4	15-20
C. Lower back (good morning, pg. 54)	2-3	8-10
D. Hamstrings (leg curl, pg. 54)	3-4	10-12

These exercises will complement your cycling, but try to work out on non-cycling days. Also you can run or skip rope to accent this activity.

BASEBALL

Muscles Needing Development:

A. Shoulders
B. Thighs
C. Calves
D. Forearms

Exercises	Sets	Reps
A. Shoulders (lateral raises, pg. 40)	3-4	10-12
B. Thighs (leg lunges, pg. 53)	3-4	10-12
C. Calves (seated calf raises, pg. 57)	3-4	15-20
D. Forearms (wrist curls, pg. 63)	3-4	12-15

Add these exercises to your normal workouts during the off-season to prepare and build yourself for your regular season. During the regular season, maintain by training twice a week with lighter weights, but increase reps.

TENNIS AND RACQUETBALL

Muscles Needing Development:

A. Forearms
B. Thighs
C. Calves
D. Stomach

Exercises	Sets	Reps
A. Forearms (wrist curls, pg. 63)	3-4	12-15
B. Thighs (leg lunges, pg. 53)	3-4	10-12
C. Thighs (squats, pg. 33)	3-4	8-10
D. Calves (seated calf raises, pg. 57)	2-3	12-15
E. Calves (standing calf raises, pg. 44)	2-3	12-15
F. Stomach (bent-leg sit-ups, pg. 48)	3-4	20-20

Overall strength is needed for racquet sports, but add these exercises to your regular program and see the difference the added strength will make in your serve and overall game. Your endurance and quickness will benefit greatly.

RUNNING (SHORT DISTANCE)

Muscles Needing Development:

A. Thighs
B. Hamstrings
C. Calves

Exercises	Sets	Reps
A. Thighs (squats, pg. 33)	3-4	8-10
B. Thighs (lunges, pg. 53)	3-4	8-10
C. Hamstrings (leg curl, pg. 54)	3-4	10-12
D. Calves (seated calf raises, pg. 57)	2-3	12-15
E. Calves (standing calf raises, pg. 44)	2-3	12-15

Overall body strength is important here, but the focus is on leg development. Another great aid to short distance running is a moderate stretching program (see chapter two). Long distance runners need little if any leg work, but should work on the upper body to maintain good overall condition.

SKIING (WATER)

Muscles Needing Development:

A. Forearms
B. Back
C. Legs
D. Biceps

Exercises	Sets	Reps
A. Forearms (wrist curls, pg. 63)	3-4	12-15
B. Back (bent over rows, pg. 41)	3-4	10-12
C. Legs (lunges, pg. 53)	3-4	8-10
D. Biceps (barbell curl, pg. 32)	2	8-10

Water skiing really requires overall development, but the exercises given here will enhance your ability. Stretching will also help improve performance.

ATHLETIC INJURIES

The great majority of injuries are caused by a lack of proper conditioning or warm-up prior to vigorous exercise. Without this warming-up period, you can expect to suffer from more strains, sprains, and muscle pulls. It's important before engaging in weight training, or any new sport, to outline a good warm-up and stretching routine. You will find that the five to ten minutes spent here will be invaluable.

Most injuries occur when a person is progressing well and becomes overconfident. This is when you usually overextend yourself and lose proper form, or overwork your muscles. So the answer here is to use common sense and progress gradually and steadily. The most common injuries that occur in weight training are to the shoulders and back. In other sports, the most frequently injured areas are the knees and elbows. There are two basic types of injuries to all these areas, and treatment is usually the same for both.

First is a simple muscle pull or muscle *strain*. This means that a few fibers have been torn in the actual muscle itself. This causes pain and swelling in the muscle, and is usually accompanied by soreness and stiffness.

The second type is of a more serious nature and is not contained within the muscle itself, but is the actual tearing of a tendon or ligament. This is called a *sprain*; a severe sprain is often worse than a broken bone. Both kinds of injuries should be treated with ice immediately, to help the numbing of pain and slow down any bleeding within the muscle that might take place. It's best to apply ice for about twenty to thirty minutes, two or three times a day, for the first couple of days after an injury, and rest it. Then begin heat treatments as well as massaging the injured area lightly, and gradually work back into your program. One important thing to remember is that this is your only body, and if there is severe pain and swelling, it could be a bad sprain and you should consult a physician.

9

Working Out at Home

Home training may be the shape of things to come. Some day, practically everyone will have a home gym, so the entire family can use the facility for better health and enjoyment.

Training at home has many advantages. It saves the cost of paying to join a health spa, it saves you time, and most of all is wonderfully convenient. The routine outlined in this chapter is designed to be done using little or no equipment. If you decide to train at home permanently, you may want to purchase a few pieces of basic equipment. For this program, all that's required is a broomstick for working the waistline and back. You may also want to purchase a pair of ankle weights, to add resistance in some of the leg exercises as you advance.

This routine is divided into three levels: beginner, intermediate, and advanced. Start at the beginner's level and gradually work your way up. Each of the three programs should be done three times a week on alternate days, e.g., Monday, Wednesday, and Friday, or Tuesday, Thursday, and Saturday.

This training program will help you get the most out of home training; as you advance, you'll probably want to personalize your program by gradually increasing the number of sets and reps, especially in the areas that need extra work. Use this program as your guideline to achieve your goals, and remember that the key to a successful exercise program is being persistent and self-motivated!

KNEE-UP

This exercise will help flatten and tighten your stomach. Sit on the floor and lean back on outstretched palms for balance. Bend at knees and tuck legs inward to your chest. (Photo 110). Push legs out to an extended position, keeping them slightly off the floor (Photo 111). Return to the starting position, with your knees to chest.

Be sure to keep your legs straight and don't touch the floor when you're in the extended position. Also, your back must be straight.

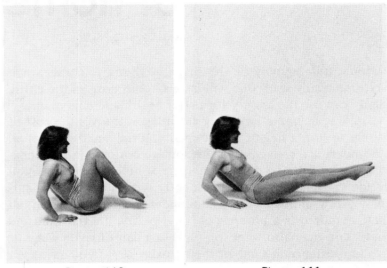

Photo 110   Photo 111

STOMACH TONER

Lie flat on the floor with your legs together and arms at your sides. Now, tuck knees in toward chest (Photo 112). Then, extend legs straight up, pointing your toes to the ceiling (Photo 113).

Keeping your back flat on the floor and stomach pulled in tight, slowly lower your legs as low as you can (but don't touch the floor) and hold for about ten seconds (Photo 114). Return to starting position with knees tucked in and repeat without stopping. Be sure to keep your spine flat on floor throughout the exercise.

Photo 112   Photo 113

Photo 114

NOSE TO KNEE SIT-UPS

This exercise is great for firming and strengthening your abdominal muscles, and your legs will also benefit. Begin by lying on the floor on your back, extend your arms overhead, and keep your feet together (Photo 115). Raise your right leg up and, at the same time, bring your upper body to a sitting position. Try to touch your ankles, bringing your nose to your knee (Photo 116). Return to starting position and repeat with your left leg; continue alternating right and left until all repetitions are completed. Be sure to keep your legs straight throughout exercise, and keep a steady pace for best results.

Photo 115   Photo 116

STANDING TWISTS

Standing twists are for trimming your hips and waist. Begin by standing with your feet comfortably apart. Place a broomstick across your shoulders, and wrap your arms around bar (Photo 117). Begin to twist at the waist as far as possible to the right (keeping your hips still), and pause (Photo 118). Now twist to your left side as far as possible and pause; continue twisting, alternating right to left. Be sure to begin slowly and then gradually speed up. Also, twist from the waist, not the hips. Proper form is always important!

REAR LEG SWING

This movement is good for working your hip and waist area. You will also feel this in the buttocks, legs, and back. Begin on your hands and knees. Extend your right leg to the side, keeping it straight and at a ninety-degree angle to your body, and look at your right foot (Photo 119).

Swing your right leg back, over to the left, and turn your head to the left, looking at your foot (Photo 120). Do all of this in the same movement. Swing right leg back to your starting position; do all repetitions without a pause, and then do your left leg. Be sure to keep your leg straight and as high as possible as you swing it.

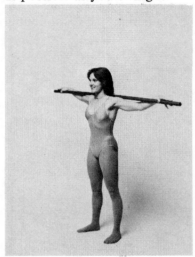

Photo 117

Photo 118

Photo 119

Photo 120

SIDE BENDS USING A BOOK

This exercise will help to trim your waistline; the book provides great resistance. Begin by standing with your feet a comfortable distance apart; place your left hand on your hip, grasp a telephone book in your right hand and extend overhead (Photo 121). Keeping your pelvis forward, bend to your left side and bounce a few times (Photo 122). Now change hands, grasping the book in your left hand, and place right hand on your hip. Then bend to your right side and bounce a few times.

Photo 121   Photo 122

BENT KNEE PUSH-UPS

This exercise will help firm and strengthen your chest area. Start on your hands and knees, with hands placed slightly wider than shoulder width apart, and fingers pointed outward. Rest on your hands, keeping knees together and head up (Photo 123).

Keeping your back straight, bend at the elbows as you slowly lower your upper body down, until chest touches the floor (Photo 124). Then, using your chest muscles, push yourself up to the starting position and repeat. Keep your upper body straight at all times and concentrate on working the chest muscles.

SHOULDER CIRCLES

This movement will firm and shape your sholders and arms. Begin by standing with your feet a comfortable distance apart and arms extended to the sides of your body at shoulder level; begin to rotate arms forward in a large circular motion. Keep your arms straight (Photo 125). Now rotate from large circles to very small circles (Photo 126). Do the same exercise, only reverse your direction and rotate arms backward. Continue at a steady pace. Concentrate on making the shoulders do the work.

GOOD MORNING

This is a great exercise for developing your lower back. It is also effective in stretching your hamstrings, the muscles in back of the thighs. Stand with a wooden bar or broomstick across your shoulders, and your feet a comfortable distance apart, holding bar with an overhand grip near the ends (Photo 127). Slowly bend forward until your upper body is parallel to the floor, back flat and head up (Photo 128). Then slowly return to starting position. Be sure to use slow and controlled movements.

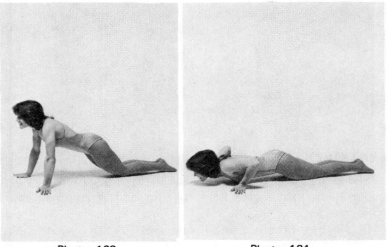

Photo 123   Photo 124

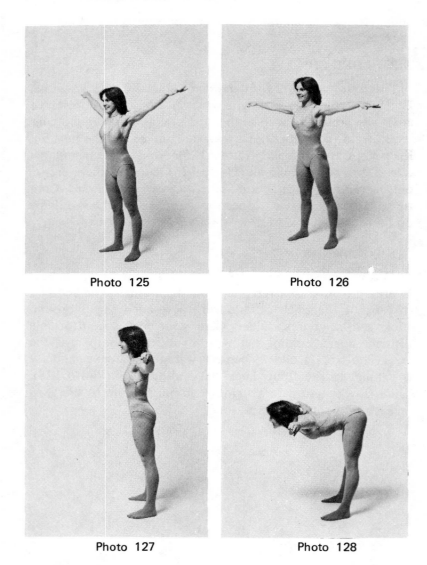

Photo 125   Photo 126

Photo 127   Photo 128

BENT-OVER PULL-UPS

These pull-ups are an excellent way to warm up your upper body. They also help to firm and strengthen your back muscles.

Begin by standing with your feet slightly wider than shoulder width apart, and bend forward from the waist until back is flat and parallel to the floor. Let arms hang down almost touching the floor, interlock your thumbs, and keep arms straight (Photo 129). Now twist your arms, shoulders, and head only to the left, pulling your left elbow upward as far and as hard as you can, and look at your elbow (Photo 130). Return to starting position with arms extended straight down. Now, repeat twisting to the right. Continue alternating right and left until all reps are done. Be sure to keep your back straight and work up gradually to a smooth, steady pace.

Photo 129   Photo 130

CHAIR TRICEP EXTENSION

This movement will help to firm the tricep muscles at the back of your upper arms. Your shoulders will also profit from this exercise.

Begin by squatting in front of a sturdy chair with your back to the seat. Place hands on the front edge, supporting your body weight (Photo 131). Bend your elbows and lower your buttocks down toward the floor as low as possible (Photo 132). Then push yourself back up, using your tricep muscles until arms are straight, and repeat. Concentrate and get a good stretch in upper arms as you go down and when you come up.

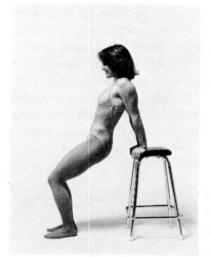 

Photo 131   Photo 132

PRONE LEG LIFTS

These leg lifts help to firm, shape, and lift your buttocks. Your legs will also be worked in this movement. Begin by lying on the floor on your stomach, with arms crossed and your chin resting on them. Legs are straight and slightly apart (Photo 133). Now raise your right leg up as high as possible (Photo 134). Lower it back down until it *almost* touches the floor (this will keep tension on the buttocks), and then raise it up again; continue this movement until the set is completed. Repeat with your left leg. Be sure to keep your legs straight and buttocks pulled in tight throughout the exercise for best results.

LEG KICKBACK

This exercise is a great way to work your buttocks, helping to firm and lift them. The legs, hips, and waist will also benefit. Begin by kneeling on the floor on your hands and knees. Tuck your right leg inward, bringing knee to chest, and drop your head to meet knee (Photo 135). Then kick your right leg to the rear and extend it as high as possible, keeping knee locked, leg straight, and head up (Photo 136); hold for a count of five. Return to starting position and continue at a steady pace until all repetitions are completed. Repeat with your left leg. Concentrate on extending each leg as high as you can. Also, keep buttocks tight throughout entire exercise.

Photo 133   Photo 134

Photo 135   Photo 136

SQUATS

Squats are good for firming and strengthening your upper thighs. Your arms will also be worked. Stand with your feet shoulder width apart and place your hands on your hips (Photo 137). Lower yourself into a squatting position, until thighs are parallel to the floor, as you bring your arms up level with your shoulders (Photo 138). Using your leg muscles, slowly push yourself back up to starting position and continue. It is important to keep your back straight and body upright. Be sure not to allow your buttocks to drop when squatting down. Keep your toes pointed slightly outward for better balance, and try to avoid raising your heels off the floor.

Photo 137   Photo 138

LEG EXTENSIONS

This movement will help to firm and shape your thighs. Using a pair of ankle weights (approximately three pounds each), strap one on each ankle. Begin by sitting on a high stool or chair, and brace yourself by holding sides of the chair with your hands, keeping your back straight at all times (Photo 139). Slowly raise right foot until your leg is fully extended and keep toes pointed (Photo 140). Now lower leg back to starting position and complete all repetitions before you start on the left leg.

It's important to use a slow, steady motion for the best results. Do not jerk the weight up. Also, get a better feel for this movement by trying it without ankle weights if you want.

MOUNTAIN CLIMBERS

Mountain climbers are excellent for firming and shaping your legs as well as increasing endurance. Your buttocks will also be worked in this movement. Begin in a lunging position with your hands on the floor, right knee up to chest, left leg extended straight back, head up (Photo 141). Now begin alternating your legs, bringing your left leg forward and extending right leg straight back (Photo 142). Continue alternating legs until all repetitions are finished. For best results, do this exercise at a fast pace.

Photo 139   Photo 140

CALF RAISES ON A BOOK

This is an excellent exercise for the calf area. To begin, stand and hold onto the back of a chair to balance yourself. Place your toes and the balls of your feet a few inches apart, on the edge of a book (toes facing forward) and let your heels drop down as far as possible (Photo 143). Now slowly rise up as high as possible on your toes and pause (Photo 144). Lower back down to starting position, pause, and continue. If you want to work the outside part of calves, point toes inward, to work inside part of calves, point toes out, and rise up and down on your toes.

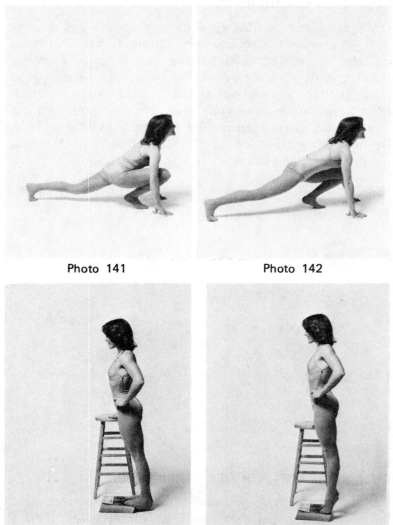

Photo 141   Photo 142

Photo 143   Photo 144

PROGRAM FOR WORKING OUT AT HOME

Exercises

Warm-ups (pg. 5)   5-10 minutes
Stretching (pg. 8)   5-10 minutes

	Beginners		Intermediate		Advanced	
	Sets	Reps	Sets	Reps	Sets	Reps
Stomach						
1. Knee-up (pg. 88)	1-2	10-15	2-3	10-20	3-4	20
2. Stomach toner (pg. 88)			2-3	10-20	3-4	20
3. Nose to knee sit-ups (pg. 89)					2-3	10-20
Hips and Waist						
1. Standing twists (pg. 90)	1-2	10-15	2	20-30	2	50
2. Rear leg swing (pg. 90)			2	10-20	3-4	20-25
3. Side bends w/book (pg. 92)			2	10-15	2-3	10-25
Chest						
1. Bent-knee push-ups (pg. 92)	1-2	8-10	2-3	10-15	3-4	15-20
Shoulders						
1. Shoulder circles (pg. 93)	1-2	10-15	2-3	10-20	3-4	20-25
Back						
1. Good morning (pg. 93)	1-2	10	2-3	10-15	3-4	10-20
2. Bent-over pull-ups (pg. 94)	1-2	10	1-2	10-15	3-4	10-20

PROGRAM FOR WORKING OUT AT HOME

Arms

Exercise	Sets	Reps	Sets	Reps	Sets	Reps
1. Chair tri extension (pg. 95)	1-2	8-10	2-3	10-15	3-4	15-20

Buttocks

Exercise	Sets	Reps	Sets	Reps	Sets	Reps
1. Prone leg lifts (pg. 96)	1-2	10-15	3	10-20	3-4	20-25
2. Leg kickbacks (pg. 96)			1-2	10-20	3	20-25

Legs

Exercise	Sets	Reps	Sets	Reps	Sets	Reps
1. Squats (pg. 98)	1-2	8-10	2-3	10-15	3	15-25
2. Leg extensions (pg. 98)			1-2	10-15	3	15-20
3. Mountain climbers (pg. 99)			1-2	10-15	3	10-20

Calves

Exercise	Sets	Reps	Sets	Reps	Sets	Reps
1. Calf raises (pg. 99)	1-2	10-15	2-3	10-20	3-4	20-25

Cool-down (pg. 16)   5 - 10 minutes

10

Couple Exercises

Exercising with a partner is a great way to get in shape! Many couples find that working out with a member of the opposite sex has unique advantages. While they are not competing with each other, they do motivate one another. Keep the routine moving, and set a comfortable pace for both of you to get an effective workout.

Begin with preliminary warm-up and stretching exercises (see Chapter 2). Get your blood flowing, limber up, and reduce any stiffness at the start. These can be done at the same time as your partner and using the same procedure, or one person can exercise while your partner assists.

Even if you both belong to a health spa or are active in a sport, two-person exercises can be an effective substitute for weight training, especially if you're traveling and don't have access to a health club. Training together will help you inspire each other, and enable you to share the results.

SIT-UPS

Sit-ups will develop your entire stomach area and help prepare you for your workout. Lying on your back, place your hands behind your head. Have your partner hold your ankles for support (Photo 145).

Now raise up as you exhale, until your elbows touch your knees (Photo 146). Slowly lower your back down to starting position while inhaling, and repeat. This is a high rep exercise and it helps to have your partner count reps for you. Also, bend your knees slightly to avoid any strain on your back.

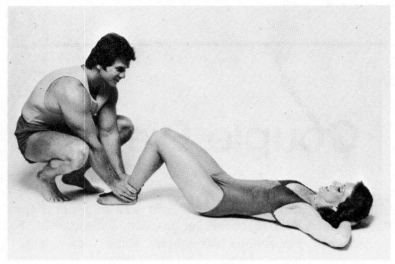

Photo 145

Photo 146

LEG RAISES

Leg raises mainly work the lower part of the stomach. This exercise will strengthen these muscles as well as help improve your posture. Start by lying on the floor with your hands under your buttocks and legs together; keep your toes pointed. (Photo 147). Bring legs up to a vertical position, using only your stomach muscles, and then have your partner apply resistance by slowly pushing them back toward the floor until you reach the starting position (Photo 148).

This is a great exercise for your stomach area, but it is not easy. You will probably start without resistance from your partner, but your strength will develop quickly and resistance will be needed.

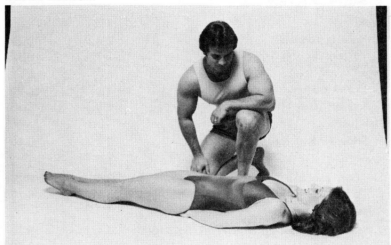

Photo 147

Photo 148

COUPLES WORKOUT PROGRAM

	Sets	Reps
Stomach		
1. Sit-ups (pg. 103)	2-4	15-25
2. Leg raises (pg. 104)	2-4	15-25
Chest		
1. Push-ups (pg. 106)	2-4	10-12
2. Chest flys (pg. 107)	2-4	10-12
Back		
1. Rowing (pg. 109)	3-4	10-12
2. Towel pulls (pg. 109)	2-3	8-10
Legs		
1. Leg extension (pg. 111)	3-4	10-12
2. Leg curl (pg. 111)	2-3	8-10
Shoulders		
1. Shoulder flys (pg. 112)	3-4	8-10
Arms		
1. Tricep extension (pg. 113)	3-4	8-10
2. Towel curls (pg. 113)	3-4	8-10
Calves		
1. Seated calf raises (intermediate) (pg. 115)	3-4	15-20
2. Donkey calf raises (advanced) (pg. 115)	3-4	15-20

PUSH-UPS

Push-ups will shape your chest area, and will strengthen your arms as well. Begin by lying face down on the floor, placing your hands slightly wider than shoulder width, and keeping legs together. Now extend your arms while having your partner place his hand on your back for resistance (Photo 149). Slowly lower yourself down, as your partner applies resistance, until you touch your chest to the floor (Photo 150). Then push yourself back up to the starting position and repeat. Keep your palms facing in and have your partner apply resistance continuously during the movement. It is also best for women to do this exercise with knees bent.

Photo 149

Photo 150

CHEST FLYS

Chest flys are effective in shaping and firming the chest. Begin by lying on your back with your arms upward and palms facing each other. Then have your training partner grasp your arms at the wrists (Photo 151). Start the movement by having your partner slowly push your arms slightly back and down until they are comfortably stretched out (Photo 152). Using only chest muscles, pull your arms back to starting position and repeat. Be sure to keep your arms slightly bent to avoid strain, and have your partner apply resistance in a slow and smooth manner.

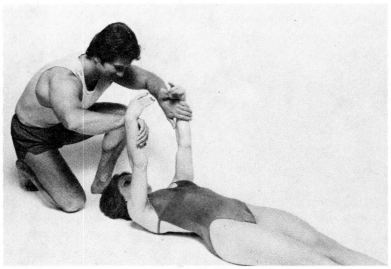

Photo 151

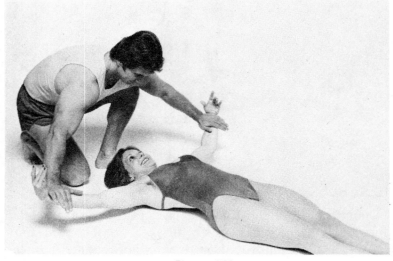

Photo 152

ROWING

Rowing is a movement to shape and strengthen your back, arms, and forearms. Sit on the floor with your legs spread and face your partner. Place a large bath towel in your hands, hold the towel in the middle, and have your partner pull his elbows to his sides while your arms are fully extended (Photo 153). Now pull your elbows back to your sides slowly, with your partner giving resistance until his arms are fully extended (Photo 154). Repeat this rowing motion until your set is complete. In the first set you should hold the towel by the middle, and then alternate with your partner in the second set.

TOWEL PULLDOWNS

Towel pulls will firm up your back and side muscles as well as add to your flexibility. Start by grabbing a towel at each end; place the center of it on a doorknob or corner of a chair. Then kneel down and lean forward to an extended position (Photo 155). Pull yourself upward and forward while bending your elbows (Photo 156). Then slowly return to

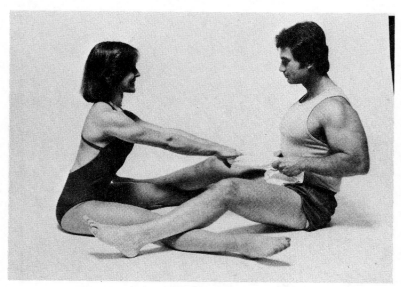

Photo 153

starting position, using the same motion, and repeat. To increase flexibility, you can stretch at the starting position with each rep. You can also have your partner give resistance by pressing on upper back during the exercise.
exercise.

Photo 154

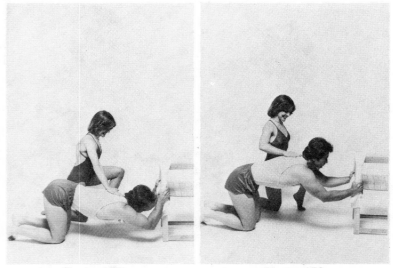

Photo 155   Photo 156

LEG EXTENSIONS

Leg extensions will shape your thighs and increase flexibility, especially around the knee. Sitting on a stool or bench, brace yourself with your hands at your sides. Bend your knee so your leg is at a ninety degree angle (Photo 157). Slowly raise your leg to a fully extended position, as your partner applies resistance by pushing against your ankle during the movement (Photo 158). Return to starting position and repeat. Be sure to move slowly and in a controlled manner throughout the movement for the best results.

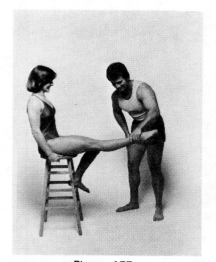
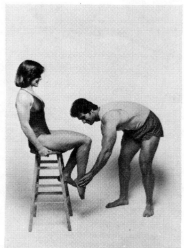

Photo 157　　　　　　　　Photo 158

LEG CURL

Leg curls work the muscles at the back of the legs, which will greatly add to the shape and contour of your legs. Lie face down with your legs together and bent back as far as possible (Photo 159). Now have your partner slowly pull your legs by the heels until they are fully extended (Photo 160). Return to starting position and repeat.

Increase resistance slowly over eight to ten workouts, keeping the reps at about eight to ten. Be sure to have your partner apply resistance smoothly throughout the entire movement.

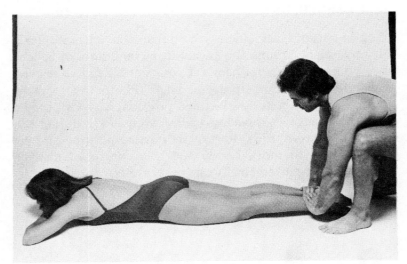

Photo 159

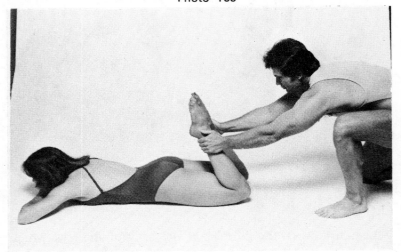

Photo 160

SHOULDER FLYS

This exercise adds to the shape and tone of the shoulder and neck muscles. Face your partner with your feet about shoulder width apart. Bend slightly at the waist and extend your arms in front of you with your palms turned down. Now have your partner hold your wrists with an overhand grip (Photo 161). Slowly raise your arms up and out to shoulder height as your partner applies resistance (Photo 162). Return to starting position in the same manner, and repeat. Keep your palms level at all times for best results, and have your partner apply resistance in both upward and downward motions.

Photo 161

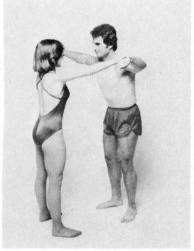
Photo 162

TRICEP EXTENSIONS

This exercise will tone the back of your upper arms and help trim excess fat in this area. Start with your back to your partner, holding a towel at each end while your partner holds the center; keep your arms bent back overhead (Photo 163). As your partner applies resistance, slowly push your arms upward until they are fully extended overhead (Photo 164). Keep the motion smooth through the movement, and try to keep your elbows as close to your head as possible for best results.

TOWEL CURLS

Towel curls will shape and tone the front of your arms. Start by facing your training partner with a towel held at each end, and your partner holding the center; keeping your arms bent and hands close to your neck (Photo 165). Now let your partner pull your arms slowly down until they are fully extended (Photo 166). Then pull your arms back up to starting position, as your partner applies resistance, and repeat. Do this movement in a controlled motion and do not allow your upper body to sway.

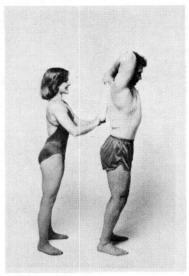

Photo 163

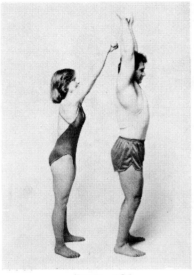

Photo 164

Photo 165

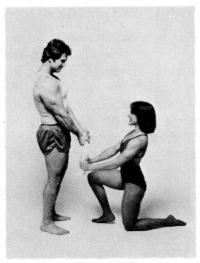

Photo 166

SEATED CALF RAISES (INTERMEDIATE)

This exercise will strengthen the entire calf, and especially shape the lower calf muscles.

While sitting on a chair, place the balls of your feet on the edge of a book or block of wood, and flex at your ankles so your calves are stretched down as far as you can go. Have your partner push down on your knees for resistance (Photo 167). Push up on your toes as high as possible as your partner applies resistance, and pause (Photo 168). Slowly lower back down to starting position and repeat. Be sure to have your training partner apply resistance at all times during this exercise for best results.

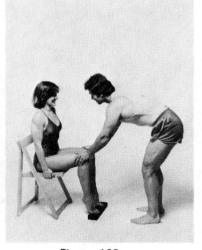

Photo 167   Photo 168

DONKEY CALF RAISES (ADVANCED)

Donkey calf raises will shape and strengthen your calves. Start by placing your feet about six inches apart on a book or a wood block. Then bend over at the waist and place your elbows on a table or bench; flex at the ankles down as far as possible. Have your partner, using a chair, sit on your lower back (Photo 169). Slowly raise up on your toes as high as you can (Photo 170). Lower back to starting position and repeat. This is a high rep exercise that is best done with as full range of movement as possible.

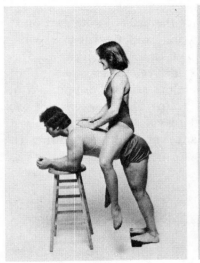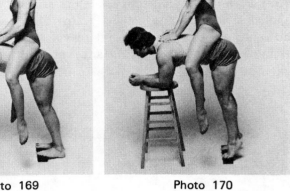

Photo 169   Photo 170

Women's Special Problems

Women actually benefit more from a physical fitness program than men do. In addition to more attractive bodies and better overall health, many physical problems derived from female anatomy are alleviated or eliminated by proper nutrition combined with progressive resistance exercises. For example, modified routines during pregnancy have been shown to be beneficial both before and after confinement and during the actual delivery.

The improvement of posture and body alignment through exercise has resulted in banishing menstrual cramps. Personal pride and self-confidence, as a result of proper mental preparation, relieve many women of the psychosomatic effects of menopause, such as melancholia and depression.

Dancers, athletes, and public figures usually appear much younger than their actual age. The obvious reason is they keep in shape. They retain a flexibility from their active lifestyles that allows them no chance to vegetate. They use their bodies and find renewed vigor. Exercise, nutrition, and a good mental attitude delay the aging process. Unused muscles will atrophy and mental laxity will fade into senility only if one consents to be the victim.

MENSTRUATION

Menstruation is a bodily function that all women have to go through. Most women, either before or during menstruation, suffer from some kind of discomfort such as cramps, headaches, nausea, lower back pain, or tenderness of the breasts. The term that is used for these discomforts is dysmenorrhea. Studies have shown that dysmenorrhea can be greatly reduced in women who are in good physical condition. Doctors have estimated that up to eighty percent of this discomfort is due to improper diet, lack of exercise, or poor posture.

The benefits of exercise and good nutrition in reducing dysmenorrhea are simple and direct. Exercising will increase the amount of oxygen in the body, which will help relieve some symptoms, while exercising the stomach and lower back muscles will greatly reduce any pain or cramps in those areas. Tension is also relieved by regular exercise.

But nutrition may be the most important factor in relieving dysmenorrhea. Every woman should know that during menstruation her body's need for iron is greatly increased; large amounts of other vitamins and minerals are needed as well. Tests have shown that calcium levels drop steadily before menstruation. This could be the cause of any feelings of depression that you may experience a few days prior to your menstrual period. It is highly recommended that you bolster your diet, especially at this time, with a good multi-vitamin and mineral supplement.

MENOPAUSE

Menopause, like most other female bodily functions, is simply a hormonal change. It is, though, greatly misunderstood and feared. The changes that occur when you stop menstruating should in no way affect your womanhood.

Menopause usually begins around the age of fifty; there is no reason it should affect a healthy woman's sex life, or overall vigor. This is one of the things about menopause that women fear. Take a positive attitude about yourself and continue to maintain an active lifestyle. Recent studies have shown that women who are active and exercise regularly have fewer problems with menopausal symptoms as well as menstruation and childbirth. Obviously, no woman can avoid these natural processes (except childbirth), but by exercising and using proper nutrition, you will have fewer problems, milder symptoms, and can enjoy a fuller and healthier life.

WEIGHT TRAINING FOR OLDER WOMEN

You are never too old to feel young. But you have to earn that feeling through an active lifestyle and proper diet. If you are out of shape, don't worry—it's never too late. But it is important that you be careful and cautious when beginning. You should consult your doctor before starting an exercise program and then allow yourself plenty of time to progress slowly and sensibly.

You will find that a consistent, well-planned exercise program will make you healthier as you begin to look and feel younger. Some problems that are often associated with getting older, such as stiff joints, shortness of breath, and poor circulation, can be greatly reduced by exercising regularly.

EXERCISE AND PREGNANCY

There has been much confusion about what effects exercise can have during pregnancy. Most research shows that there are few reasons why a woman shouldn't exercise during and after pregnancy.

Naturally, women should use a common-sense approach to their exercising. Weight control and keeping your stomach muscles in good condition are the two main benefits from exercising during pregnancy. Recent studies have indicated that physically active women who become pregnant experience fewer complications during pregnancy and delivery than women who are not in good physical condition. These women have better breathing control and stronger stomach muscles which help produce shorter labor.

Exercise during pregnancy should be modified to suit the individual, and should be done under the guidance of your physician. The time to start exercising is before you get pregnant, not after. Being in good physical condition will greatly reduce any possible risks during pregnancy. Be sure to talk with your doctor before continuing your regular exercise program.

Other advantages of exercising during pregnancy are the easing of lower back pain and increased vitality. Staying in good condition before giving birth also makes it easier to get back in shape after giving birth. As you progress during pregnancy, and your weight is increasing, you will need better strength in your stomach and lower back muscles for added support. Some women also experience an enlarging of their breasts. This can make you hunch your shoulders; it would be good to do some exercises for your shoulders, upper back, and chest.

I've often been asked by pregnant women for suggestions on how to avoid those ugly stretch marks. Almost all health food stores carry various Vitamin E creams. Apply one of these creams after bathing, especially to your stomach and breasts, to help avoid such marks. If you are unable to find a high-potency Vitamin E cream, buy regular Vitamin E capsules and add the oil inside them to your own cream. Vitamin E will work wonders on your skin and will give it the elasticity it needs to stretch without any damage.

POSTURE

Posture refers to the basic structural alignment of the human body. Good posture is very important for your health as well as your appearance. No matter how well you develop your body, if you do not have good posture, you will not look attractive.

Poor posture can be caused by several factors. The most common is simply laziness, which can be easily corrected. You should always make a point of walking in an upright stance, keeping your shoulders back, holding your head straight and your stomach pulled in. Another cause of bad posture is much more serious, and is due to abnormalities of the spine. The majority of these are inherited or caused by occupational and personal habits. Problems of this nature should be referred to a physician; he or she can either recommend a good specialist or outline specific exercises to help correct these problems.

Some activities, hobbies, or sports have a negative effect on your posture. This does not mean that you have to give them up. All you need to do is become more aware of your posture at all times, and work on improving it by doing a few exercises about three times a week. This will keep your good muscles from becoming lazy and will help to strengthen weak ones. Before you start to work on improving your posture, it is a good idea to stop and take note of the area or areas that could use improving. Begin by standing sideways in front of a full-length mirror. Now as you're standing sideways, draw an imaginary line from your ear to the front of your ankle. If your posture is correct, the line should pass through the shoulder joint, hip joint, and knee joint. Any of these points that do not fall into line need to be worked on so they are back to normal. The longer a posture problem goes unattended, the harder it will be to correct.

Here's a tip to help improve your posture which can be practiced most every day. Begin by remembering to make a point of using perfect posture every time you drive your car. Place both your hands on the steering wheel, keep your back straight, stomach in, and shoulders back. Since most people complain that they don't have enough time to work on their posture, this should be a great help!

The following exercises will help to improve your posture if done correctly and consistently. As with stretching exercises, you should begin with the easier movements and gradually progress to the more advanced ones. If you have doubts or problems about your physical condition, I suggest you consult a physician before starting.

POSTURE EXERCISE

This is a good basic exercise that will start you on the way to better posture. Begin by sitting on the floor with your legs crossed and hands resting on your thighs. Breathe slowly and deeply to a count of five as you inhale; hold for five and then take a count of five as you exhale. Remember that this can be done easily while watching television, reading, or any other time you can (Photo 171).

LUMBAR

Here is another excellent exercise that can be done easily. Begin by lying flat on your back on the floor; slowly raise your knees to your chest and gently hold thighs against stomach, bringing your head up. Hold this position for about a minute. Then slowly bring your legs back down and repeat. After you become comfortable in this position, begin holding it for a longer period of time. I'm sure you will find this not only helps your posture, but can be very relaxing (Photo 172).

It's very important that you keep your back completely flat on the floor throughout the entire exercise.

CERVICAL

To begin this exercise sit on a chair in an upright position and clasp your hands together behind your head; keep your chin pointed down and elbows up high (Photo 173). Slowly apply resistance against your head with hands and hold for a count of five. Now gradually release pressure, relax, and repeat ten times. Another good way to do this movement is by placing your back to a wall. Be sure to keep your back straight at all times.

DORSAL

Begin by lying on your stomach with your chin resting on the floor, and clasp your hands together behind your lower back (Photo 174). Now raise your head and upper chest, and both legs at the same time, by arching your back (Photo 175). Hold this position for a slow count of five, then lower slowly

Photo 171   Photo 172

back to starting position and repeat. Work up to ten repetitions. This is an advanced movement, so be sure to work into
it slowly and increase repetition gradually.

Photo 173, top left
Photo 174, center
Photo 175, bottom

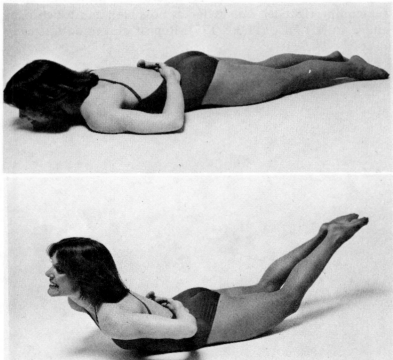

The rest of this book is devoted to helping to shape and firm a woman's most common problem areas: the stomach, buttocks, legs, hips, and waist. If you feel you have a problem in any of these areas, add a few of these exercises to your regular program. These additional exercises will greatly increase your progress and will enhance any weight control program you may be following. I'm sure you will be happy with the results you will achieve.

LYING STEAM ENGINE

This movement works your stomach to help tighten and strengthen it, and also develops your legs, back, and waistline. Lie on your back, hands behind your head with your fingers interlocked. Legs together flat on the floor. Pull your right knee up toward your chest, twist upper body, and touch left elbow to your right knee (Photo 176), extended leg out. Now alternate and bring left knee up toward chest (extending right leg out as far as possible), and touch right elbow to left knee (Photo 177). Repeat at a smooth, steady pace.

Photo 176   Photo 177

SPREAD LEG SIT-UP

Your stomach will be worked in this exercise. You will also feel a stretch in the back of your legs and back muscles. Lie on your back with arms extended overhead and your legs spread far apart (Photo 178). Raise torso to sitting position and reach with both arms toward left foot, trying to touch toes with fingertips (Photo 179). Lie back down (using a steady pace). Raise torso back up and reach straight forward between the legs, arms straight. Lie down and repeat for your right foot.

Photo 178   Photo 179

JACKKNIFE SIT-UP

This is a great exercise for tightening the entire stomach area. It also improves your coordination and balance. Lie on your back, with arms extended overhead; legs straight and together (Photo 180). Keeping your legs straight, raise them both and at the same time raise your upper body to a pike position. Try to touch toes with your fingers while in this position (Photo 181). Lower yourself back to starting position, and do all repetitions without pause.

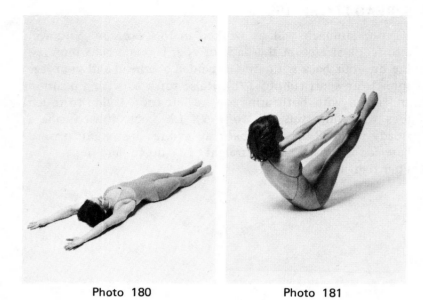

Photo 180   Photo 181

SCISSORS

The scissors will work the entire abdominal area, firming and reducing it. Lie on your back with legs together and hands at your sides. Raise your legs together so that your toes are pointed toward the ceiling; open legs wide (Photo 182) and close them, scissor-like, ten times. Now, lower legs until they're about six inches off the floor, open legs wide (Photo 183), and close them, repeating scissors another ten times. Let legs down to floor and relax.

CRUNCH

This exercise firms and flattens the stomach. Lie on your back with knees bent in, feet flat on the floor, fingers interlaced under head, and elbows up (Photo 184). In one smooth movement, sit up and bring elbows forward to touch your knees (Photo 185). Slowly roll back down to starting position.

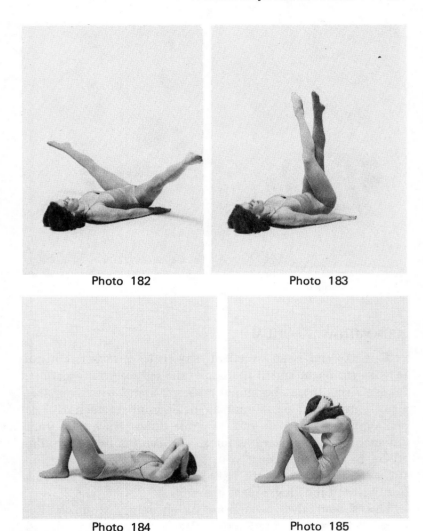

Photo 182   Photo 183

Photo 184   Photo 185

CONTRACT AND RELEASE

This exercise is mainly for your stomach, but it will also help strengthen the back and neck muscles. Begin in a kneeling position. Drop your head between your arms, pull stomach in tight, and round your back up; hold (Photo 186). Now release, bringing head up; lift your buttocks high and arch your back (Photo 187) and repeat.

Photo 186   Photo 187

ABDOMINAL VACUUM

This exercise is an excellent way to learn muscle control in your stomach, and at the same time reduce your waistline. It also firms these abdominal muscles. Stand with your feet slightly apart and place your hands on your stomach. Exhale and empty all the air out of your lungs. Now suck your stomach in and upward as far as you can (as though you're trying to touch it against your spine) and hold this position for a count of ten (Photo 188). Relax, letting your stomach out. Without inhaling, repeat exercise.

This should always be done on an empty stomach. Remember to exhale completely before sucking stomach in and keep your lungs empty throughout this exercise. Try doing this in front of a mirror; it helps concentration to watch yourself.

KNEELING LEG LIFTS (TO THE SIDE)

This is an excellent exercise for trimming your hip and waist area. Begin by kneeling on your hands and knees.

Extend your right leg out to the side, keeping your leg straight and head up (Photo 189). Now lower your leg and touch your toe to the floor (Photo 190). Then raise it upward as high as possible, keeping head up. Repeat at a steady pace until the desired number of repetitions are completed, and then do the same with your left leg.

Photo 188

Photo 189

Photo 190

FAN KICK

This movement works your waist, legs, and buttocks. Lie on your side and support your body with your hands; keep legs straight and together (Photo 191). Lift leg up and swing it in front of body (Photo 192), then to the side (Photo 193), and now behind your body (Photo 194). Let these movements flow in half-circular motions. Roll over on buttock and do the other side, after completion of all repetitions on this side.

Photo 191	Photo 192

Photo 193	Photo 194

WAIST TWIST

This exercise will help reduce your waist. Stand with your feet slightly wider than shoulder width apart, with arms extended at shoulder level (Photo 195). Then twist trunk to the right as far as possible, pause, and twist to the right again (Photo 196). Return to center and repeat on the left.

Photo 195   Photo 196

KNEELING LEG KICKBACK WITH CURL

This is an excellent exercise for working your buttocks, hips, waist, legs, and lower back. Begin by kneeling on your hands and knees. Tuck your right leg inward, bringing knee to chest and dropping your head to meet knee (Photo 197). Kick your right leg to the rear as high as possible, keeping leg straight, knee locked, and head up (Photo 198); hold for a count of five. Now keep your thigh still and curl lower part of your leg toward buttocks; pause (Photo 199) and straighten leg again. Return to starting position and continue at a steady pace until ten repetitions are completed. Repeat with your left leg. Be sure to lift your leg as high as possible. Also, keep buttocks tight throughout entire movement.

Photo 197   Photo 198

Photo 199

PRONE LEG LIFTS

This exercise will help to firm and shape your buttocks. It also works the lower back and legs.

Begin on the floor, lying on your stomach, with your arms crossed and chin resting on them, legs straight and a little apart (Photo 200). Raise your right leg up as high as you can (Photo 201), lower it until it *almost* touches the floor, and then raise it up again. (This will keep tension on the buttocks.) Continue until set is completed and repeat with left leg.

For best results, keep leg straight and buttock pulled in tight throughout the movement.

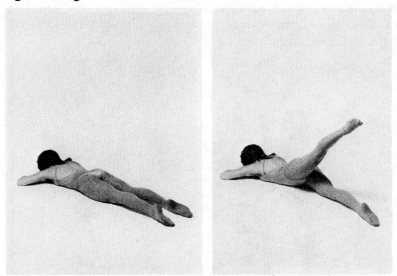

Photo 200   Photo 201

STANDING LEG LIFTS

Here is another great exercise for firming your legs and buttocks. Begin by standing with one arm resting on the back of a chair for balance, with your weight on your inside leg. Rest your outside leg lightly on the floor, with toes pointed slightly behind your body. Lift your outside leg to the rear as high as possible (Photo 202), lower to floor, and pause. Then lift your outside leg to the front as high as possible (Photo 203), and lower back to floor. Continue this movement at a steady pace. It's important to use good posture; keep your body upright throughout the entire exercise.

HINDU-JUMPS

Here's another excellent exercise for firming your buttocks and legs, as well as increasing your endurance. Begin this movement with your feet a comfortable distance apart and

your hands on hips (Photo 204). Squat down until legs go below parallel and extend arms out in front of you for balance
(Photo 205). From this position, jump up until your feet rise
above the floor, keeping toes pointed (Photo 206). Return to
squatting position and repeat in a continuous motion.

This is an advanced exercise, so be sure to begin with just
a few repetitions and increase gradually as your strength
and endurance improve.

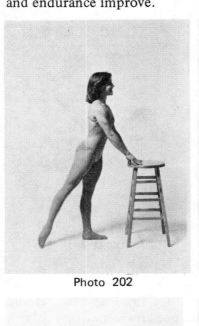

Photo 202

Photo 203

Photo 204

Photo 205

Photo 206

PRONE LEG SCISSORS

Here is another exercise to help firm your buttocks and strengthen your back and legs.

Begin by lying on your stomach on the floor, and place your hands under your pelvis to help cushion yourself. Keeping your legs together and straight, lift them off the floor as high as you can (Photo 207). Open your legs as far as possible, keeping your knees locked; begin by crossing your left leg over the right (Photo 208). Continue by opening legs wide again; this time cross your right leg over left. Repeat in a scissor-like movement.

BOTTOMS-UP

This is an excellent exercise for working your buttocks and legs. Begin by assuming a common push-up position, with legs straight and together (Photo 209). While keeping your legs together, hop toward your hands as far as possible, bringing buttocks up high as you tuck your head under (Photo 210).

Then hop back to starting position and repeat using a smooth continuous motion.

To get the full benefits from this exercise, it's important to remember to keep your legs together and straight throughout.

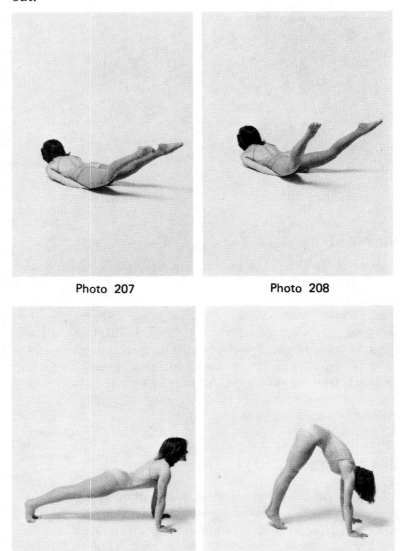

Photo 207   Photo 208

Photo 209   Photo 210

4-COUNT SQUATS

This is an excellent way to firm and shape your legs and buttocks.

First, stand with your feet about shoulder width apart, toes pointed slightly outward, and your hands on your hips (Photo 211). Lower yourself down into a squatting position and place your arms inside your legs, with hands flat on the floor (Photo 212). Raise your buttocks up as far as you can and try to straighten your legs, keeping your fingertips on the floor (Photo 213). Lower back to your squatting position and return to starting position, and repeat.

Begin this exercise slowly; when you feel comfortable with each movement, gradually pick up the pace.

Photo 211, top left
Photo 212, top right
Photo 213, bottom

BACK KICKS

This is another excellent exercise for working the buttocks and legs.

Lie on the floor on your right side, legs straight and together, and support upper body with your hands (Photo 214).

Now kick your left leg to the back, using short, sharp kicks in a quick continuous motion (Photo 215). Then roll over on your left side and repeat on your right leg.

Concentrate on making the buttocks do the work in this movement.

Photo 214   Photo 215

SIDE LYING STRAIGHT KICKS

This will help firm your buttocks, legs and waist.

Lie on the floor on your left side; keep legs straight and together, and support yourself with your hands (Photo 216).

Now kick your right leg straight up toward your head as far as possible, while keeping knees locked and toes pointed up to ceiling (Photo 217).

Photo 216   Photo 217

About the Author

EDIE LEEN is a weight training instructor, dancer, and model who lives in Foster City, California. She is a former Miss Bay Area, and was helped in the writing of this book by her husband ED BERTLING, owner of the Monarch Health Club, San Bruno, California.

Index

NEW BOOKS FOR WOMEN FROM ANDERSON WORLD

Runner's World Yoga Book

By Jean Couch with Nell Weaver. Couch, a respected international instructor, has written what is rapidly becoming the most popular book of its kind. The more than 300 photos and a step-by-step approach enable novice and intermediate alike to rapidly attain flexibility while improving posture and skin tone. 220 pages. $11.95.

Total Woman's Fitness Guide

By Gail Shierman, Ph.D. and Christine Haycock, M.D. Physical fitness programs designed to your lifestyle. How do sports and activities keep you trim? What areas do they affect first . . . and most? Get the most from your favorite activity. Get the most from your life. With charts for self-evaluation and programs for fitness. 144 pages. $4.95.

Women's Gymnastics

By Jack Wiley. A complete, all-around guide to women's gymnastics. Standard exercises are amply illustrated in sequence and carefully explained along with rules, scoring, judging, organizations, and clubs. 176 pages. $6.95.

Natural Foods Cookbook

By Pamela Hannan. More than 300 taste-tested and proven recipes designed to eliminate both refined sugar and preservatives from your diet. Plus a chapter on combining foods for maximum nutritional value with an emphasis on breads, pastries, and rolls. $12.95.

Dance Aerobics

By Maxine Polley. Two words best describe Dance Aerobics—fitness and expression. An exciting, enjoyable way to stay slim while at the same time developing balance, grace, and style. Polley explains routines, warm-up, cool-down, plus expression with varied musical tempos. 160 pages. $5.95.

Women's Soccer Guide

By Valerie Tucker. Tucker, a player and former *Soccer World* editor, has compiled this unique volume solely with the woman player in mind. Every aspect of the game is covered from the penalty kick, position playing and ball-handling skills to tactics, rules, and the fundamentals of teamwork. 140 pages. $3.95.

Getting in Control of Your Weight

By David W. Abbott, Ph.D. All those diets and none of them have worked? It may not be the food, but you. Dr. Abbott has combined calorie-burning nutrition plans with behavior modification techniques that will help you lose, control, and maintain your desired weight. 140 pages. $4.95.

Skin Care for Men and Women Outdoors

By Cameron Smith, M.D. Don't let the outdoors age you prematurely. Dr. Smith, a dermatologist, shows you his secrets for keeping smooth, youthful looking skin despite the sun and elements. Plus, how to care for minor scrapes, insect bites, allergies, and minimize scarring. 272 pages. $12.95.

The Complete Woman Runner

By the Editors of *Runner's World*. An athletic guide written expressly for women. Don't settle for finding what you can in a man's book. This hardback edition gives you up-to-date advice on everything from your first step out the door to your first step across the finish line. 440 pages. $10.95.

A Woman's Self-Defense Manual

By Michael G.V. Pickering. Do fears of physical harassment limit your life? Does darkness force you indoors? Get some confidence, learn self-defense. Easy-to-learn methods to neutralize attackers and reduce chances of assualt. 144 pages. $5.95.

☐ Please rush me the women's book I've marked below! I've included my check or money order. *Please add $1 each for postage and handling. Calif. residents add 6% sales tax.*

I can't wait for the mail.

If not, please call toll-free 800/227-8318 (in California 800/982-6133) and have your order filled today.

☐ Runner's World Yoga Book	ISBN 206-3	$11.95	$_____
☐ Total Woman's Fitness Guide	ISBN 163-6	$ 4.95	$_____
☐ Women's Gymnastics	ISBN 223-3	$ 6.95	$_____
☐ Natural Foods Cookbook	ISBN 208-X	$12.95	$_____
☐ Dance Aerobics	ISBN 186-5	$ 5.95	$_____
☐ Women's Soccer Guide	ISBN 221-7	$ 3.95	$_____
☐ Getting in Control of Your Weight	ISBN 187-3	$ 4.95	$_____
☐ Skin Care for Men and Women Outdoors	ISBN 148-2	$12.95	$_____
☐ The Complete Woman Runner	ISBN 143-1	$10.95	$_____
☐ A Woman's Self-Defense Manual	ISBN 166-0	$ 5.95	$_____

Postage and Handling $_____

Calif. state sales tax $_____

☐ Anderson World Catalog ($.50) $_____

Total Amount $_____

Send to:

Anderson World, Inc., 1400 Stierlin Road, Mountain View, CA 94043